1974

Edinburgh Bilingual Library (2)

The *purpose* of this series is to study the words and comprehend the meaning of works by poets, playwrights, and prose writers that express the creative consciousness of Europe at periods of great vitality.

The *method* is that of facing text and translation, prefaced by original critical assessments, and followed by annotation appropriate to Honours student level.

The *structure* of the series is thematic. The books group into related studies of subject matter and styles. Among the early groups are:

1 The *amour courtois* tradition from the troubadours to the neo-platonists.
2 Renaissance and later reworking of classical mythology. This group will contain medieval Latin drama, Italian renaissance drama, Poliziano, Góngora, Tasso, Calderón, Lope de Vega, Racine, etc.
3 The gothic imagination of the 19th century and after. Here we will explore the 'romantic agony' and its post-Freudian aftermath in 20th-century existentialism and the theatre of the absurd.
4 Symbolism, surrealism, and other 20th-century styles.

By such means, the barriers imposed by language upon literature will be transcended. A student of Shakespeare will be able to know Lope de Vega; a student of French to compare Calderón and Racine; a student of German contrast Goethe and Foscolo. Perhaps even more important, all readers will be able to follow the thread theory of creative ideas, winding and evolving in country after country, over the centuries.

EDINBURGH BILINGUAL LIBRARY (2)

Phèdre

JEAN RACINE

Phaedra

EDITED AND TRANSLATED BY
R. C. KNIGHT
Professor of French
University College of Swansea

UNIVERSITY OF TEXAS PRESS, AUSTIN

International Standard Book Number 0-292-76403-0
Library of Congress Catalog Card Number 79-38577
© 1971 by R. C. Knight

Printed in Great Britain by
W & J Mackay & Co Ltd, Chatham, Kent

Contents

IN MEMORIAM E.M.K.

Phèdre
Racine

INTRODUCTION

Racine tells us that this play is adapted from one by Euripides. But the statement, like many in his prefaces, needs interpreting in the light of facts that he has seen fit to conceal, and of critical notions that had not been reached in his time.

In the first place, his play is original, in the only sense that makes sense: he took what he liked and made of it what he wished; he had felt, imaginatively, all he wrote. But because we know some of the sources (several besides Euripides), we can learn interesting things about his attitude to his subjects, and at the same time interesting things about the different tragic arts of Athens and Paris.

Thus, while he was the only Greek scholar writing for the theatre, and one of the 'party of the Ancients' in the current controversy, and therefore proud of owing a debt to Euripides, he was much less proud of an equal debt—whether in terms of situations or lines of verse—to the Roman tragedian Seneca, and quite unwilling to refer to the not inconsiderable use he had made of French plays on this subject written in his own century.

If we compare the two very great tragedies, the Greek *Hippolytus* and *Phèdre*, it must not be to assign an order of merit. (The Latin *Phaedra* we can safely put below both.) In Euripides' play Hippolytus was the hero, and the woman who loved him was the, so to speak, accidental victim of a goddess's grudge against him. It is a powerful play, and must have been disturbing to any true believer in the Greek pantheon. 'Venus, to excuse Phaedra, says she made her fall in love', Racine noted in the margin of the speech with which this goddess (the Aphrodite of Euripides) opens the tragedy: it does excuse her to a great extent, although—like Oedipus—she is the first to acknowledge as wicked the passion into which she has fallen. The youth, then, slights the goddess of love, for motives we may call religious, since he has a mystic bond with another goddess, the chaste patroness of hunting. The goddess strikes at him through the adulterous passion of his stepmother (adulterous, but not incestuous, in Athenian eyes). Approached by her nurse, he is outraged. Phaedra hangs herself after writing an accusation of rape against him for her absent husband Theseus to find on his return. The sea-god sends a dragon at Theseus' prayer, which causes Hippolytus' death. Carried home, he dies on stage, but first is reconciled to his father by his patroness Artemis. *He* is the tragic hero— guilty of *hubris* (against the goddess, but also against Phaedra by his uncomprehending puritanism) and punished by *nemesis* beyond his deserts. The title is *Hippolytus*. His death is the dénouement, whereas Phaedra dies midway through the action. She has one long scene of great pathos and beauty, interrupted by the invectives of Hippolytus (who does not see her), and dies pitied by us, the readers or the audience, in spite of her calumny. A most moving episode, but an episode. Her suffering is over before that of her victim begins.

However, in an earlier *Hippolytus* of Euripides of which the text is lost, Phaedra had had a different role, and presumably a less passive one, since we know it shocked the public. Scholars think some of it is preserved in the tragedy of Seneca.

The Roman Phaedra, in the rhetorical style of Senecan tragedy, declares with force that she hates her guilty desire; but once her nurse has dissuaded her from death she goes to find Hippolytus, faints in his arms and then pleads for his love. (By Roman law this *would* be incest.) In this version she lives longer, and stabs herself over the young man's corpse, after telling her husband the truth (as only she can, since Seneca brings no deities on to his stage). Her portrait is here much coarser, though more energetic; and she claims at least half the tragic interest, since in this version not he but she, with all her house, is hated by the goddess. She appears in four of the five acts, and hers is the death nearest to the close of the play.

Seneca was the model for the renaissance plays on Phaedra, not Euripides: *his* Greek was too hard for most men of letters —and who reads Greek poetry in Latin translations? The

French seventeenth century saw several more *Hippolytes*, which drifted further and further from their starting-point as the century progressed.[1] For out of the renaissance rules of art which went to form *la doctrine classique* this age had greatly increased the scope of one, which is called *la bienséance* or *les bienséances*—the idea of what is proper and fitting. Characters should be like the reality, or simply suitable, says Aristotle's *Poetics*; which the critic D'Aubignac paraphrased in 1657 by saying that a king in a play should behave like a real king. But this could mean that Corneille's Auguste was expected to behave like Louis XIII, and Racine's Thésée like Louis XIV, with all the etiquette of the Louvre; or, more seriously, that 'unless the subject conforms to the manners and ideas of the audience'—to quote D'Aubignac again—'it will never succeed.' Three things in this Phaedra story shocked the growing squeamishness of the Paris public, which was far more censorious about art than life—a married heroine with a sinful passion (as in so many novels of more recent times), a false accusation of rape, and worst of all, a young man who would not or could not love a woman. Unfortunately these are the three essentials of the plot. So all they could do was to write new stories about an unmarried princess called Phèdre unhappily in love with a decent polite young man called Hippolyte, who in one version actually loves her in return, and in another has his own secret love-affair (as he still has in Racine; for we observe that he dared not flout public taste in this particular—the love interest was expected, and a hero indifferent to the other sex would have invited ribald comment). They kept the names, and kept the fish-tailed bull who comes to end Hippolyte's life (in the wings); but he does seem rather out of place in their china-shops.

It showed courage in Racine to put back as much of the old story as he did. True, his Hippolyte is charged with no more than an attempt on Phèdre; true, he is in love—but everybody in the play looks on him as the rough ascetic that Euripides had shown. (And Racine has given him a beloved as worthy of himself as he could devise, and who only comes on the stage twice. This love moreover is, in a very minor degree, a guilty passion too, and forms, if we observe it closely and sympathetically, a delicate prelude and parallel to that of Phèdre.) But now once again the undoubted centre of the play—with the longest, intensest, most poetic role he ever wrote, one that has often been said to unbalance the total impression—is a married woman, and her sinful desire is the subject of the tragedy.

We may say that Racine took from Euripides the character of his Phèdre—essentially virtuous, yearning for purity, victim of a goddess (though in the French play we have only her word for this)—and from Seneca her lustful acts. This is a contradiction, but the whole conception of the character is a contradiction and always had been—the sinner who hates her sin, *Phèdre malgré soi perfide, incestueuse* as Boileau puts it; and the contradiction is a fact, a painful fact, of human nature.

His heroine does more, or at least suffers, plans, reacts more than even Seneca's figure; for a modern play has a fuller action than any ancient tragedy, where the choruses take up so much of the acting time or written pages. What Racine has done is to space out the essential scenes his sources gave him. In Act I Phèdre confesses her sin to her nurse (as in Euripides), in Act II, to Hippolyte (as in Seneca); at the beginning of Act IV Thésée, who returned in Act III, denounces his son (Euripides); in Act V the tale of Hippolyte's death draws on both. What lies between the great moments is: first, of course, the few scenes devoted to Aricie and Hippolyte; and for the rest, scenes of foreboding or recollection in which Phèdre dwells on her predicament: now hoping, and forgetting her conscience, now remembering, and loathing herself. One of these original scenes, one which could not have existed but for the invented rival Aricie, is itself a great moment, perhaps the greatest in the play (the end of Act IV).

Modern critics, at least in Britain, tend to feel that the forms of the drama Racine wrote, and therefore its tone, need explaining away, since it is a fact that they are obsolete now and could not be revived by any living dramatist.

I would not wish to lay too much stress on the concept of 'French classicism', or on the 'rules' as they tend to appear to our anarchistic age. Racine held no theories about classicism, and never heard the word; moreover the quite opposite set of tendencies that criticism is coming to highlight for preference, especially on the continent—the sense of stress and conflict, the preoccupation with the showy, the evanescent, the illusory, those ill-defined and perhaps ill-assorted features that go under the name of the baroque—give no doubt as true a picture of Racine's age as the 'classical' picture they seek to replace.

The age did believe that there must be rules, and that it must be wise, before you write, to know what they are; because it used the word art without a capital letter, in exactly the same sense as when we still speak of the arts of war or angling—it was the know-how of a difficult pursuit (the word, derived from the Latin *ars*, translated the Greek τέχνη), and it was better to find out the short-cuts that were known than to waste time in trial and error. 'It is agreed that there are precepts, since there is an art,' said Racine's great predecessor and rival Corneille; though he, having an abnormally independent mind, went on 'but it is not agreed what they are.'

The formulations of the seventeenth century, as regards drama (or indeed art in general) seem crude to us because no special vocabulary, and in fact no special concepts, had yet been developed. The first work which ever attempted a reasoned inquiry into the nature of literature—the only work of the kind surviving from before the renaissance, Aristotle's *Poetics*—had only been re-discovered by scholarship just before 1500, and it proved a very hard nut to crack. It gave the sixteenth and seventeenth centuries two key notions, each of which evolved in ways their author had never intended—*bienséance*, of which something has been said already, and *vraisemblance*, or verisimilitude, by which Aristotle had meant a credibility depending either upon public belief in a story or on a causal nexus, 'probable or necessary' as the English translations put it, between successive events in the action of a play, especially as regards the dénouement, or between the character of the doer and the things he is made to do.

But to a certain Castelvetro, writer of an Italian commentary on the *Poetics* in 1570, who influenced French poets of the Pléiade period and again in the seventeenth century, verisimilitude meant making the dramatic performance itself (and not the action it represented) seem credible and indeed real to the audience. He and his followers believed, and no doubt it was natural enough at the time, that the moment the audience has 'occasion to reflect on what it sees and doubt its reality', it cannot feel the emotions proper to drama. The principal consequences were the 'unities'—the 'unity of time' limiting the scenic action to 'one revolution of the sun' (an illogical compromise: one would have expected simply the two-and-a-half hours or so which it took to watch the play—but this would have been asking too much, and the other formula is in the *Poetics*); and the 'unity of place', forbidding at first a shift from country to country or city to city, and only later, but before Racine, from room to room—however, a lot of sleight of hand was always indulged in here.

In fact in Greece and Rome, in so far as the question of place or time was ever posed, these limits had usually been observed; the perpetual presence of a chorus on the stage made it difficult not to. They had dictated the form of *Hippolytus* and *Phaedra*, so Racine had no particular problem here. No stage could ever exhibit the death of the hero as legend had depicted it; and Racine's description, though it has always been attacked as over-elaborate, only needs to be well spoken to hold the audience to the last word. As for time, Racine is able to establish the past of Phèdre, Hippolyte and Thésée in sufficient detail. Only critical reflexion detects that the false report of Thésée's death, and then his return, come in rather too conveniently; but what they really do is to articulate and precipitate phases in Phèdre's crisis which are probable and acceptable enough in themselves, though without such help they would have demanded a leisurely time-scheme such as a novelist, or Shakespeare, would have arranged for them.

Shakespeare's countrymen may have particular difficulty in believing that there are any compensating virtues in this hopeless pursuit of hundred-per-cent stage illusion—quite hopeless, if we realize the crudity of their theatrical arrangements; and any way, the characters spoke in French, and spoke in verse. But surely an age like ours which has welcomed and played with so many sorts of experimental theatre needs no special apology for this one. Its advantages have long been a commonplace of French criticism. The doctrine of verisimilitude included sensible minor rules like the insistence on a stated and plausible motive, except at beginnings of acts, for every entrance and exit (note Phèdre's at the beginning, and Thésée's at the end, of IV iv). But above all it had a (fortuitous) result which Racine must have clearly realized (unless it simply never occurred to him to do anything different)—it eliminated all but the essentials, suppressed all side-issues and irrelevancies, and concentrated a fierce light on the final movements of an action which was forced to become, as Goethe called it, a crisis.

The tone of the play too is confined to a much narrower gamut than Shakespeare has accustomed us to: the seventeenth century thought that any perceptible contrast would have created discord. But Racine knows all about the need for intervals of lowered tension, and he must have intended the hidden smile, the contraband touches of comedy, that illuminate Hippolyte's awakening to love.

In one important respect (which is not a 'rule' at all) Racine's age was already on the modern side of a great watershed. The commercial Paris theatre of the first half-century had brought into tragedy, from comedy and the bastard genre of tragi-comedy, something it had never been conscious of before—the need to keep the audience in its seats by keeping it in suspense about the dénouement. Euripides had been so far from feeling this that he commonly announced the dénouements of his tragedies in their prologues. The new discovery was undoubtedly influential, but it laid stress on the cheaper kinds of dramatic emotion. It is possible to notice that Racine remembers the principle, from reminders inserted mostly at the ends of acts: but in *Phèdre* our main response is certainly not to this, but to something profounder and much more difficult to compass, the imaginative exploring of emotion and pain.

The characters, like those in the play's classical models, are extremely exalted in social status, or else humble, deferential and increasingly faceless as their role becomes less important. They include, more often than ancient tragedy, the utility character called the confidant (of either sex), who calls forth information by questions, turns monologue into dialogue, and sometimes expresses one voice in the interior debate of the character to which he is attached. His primary characteristics—his only characteristics almost—are to be completely discreet, completely trusted, and not more than averagely intelligent (since he puts the audience's questions for them) and to have no character or concerns (so far as we ever hear) of his own. A useful device, conventional but not implausible, for the great ones of the earth do, or did, have such dependents and counsellors; one which Racine is careful not to overdo—Thésée has no confidant, Œnone and Théramène have some individuality and some personal status, only Ismène is so colourless as to be practically invisible.

The other features that bear the mark of their date and place are matters of production. I should not recommend the modern reader to try to imagine *Phèdre* just as it was put on the stage of the Hôtel de Bourgogne in 1677, nor would I recommend a modern producer to try to reproduce the set of 1677 exactly. It was abstract only in the sense that it would have served for many other tragedies—and probably had; though the designer did attempt to indicate arches of some kind ('un palais voûté', we read in his notebook which has been preserved), presumably with line 854 in mind (872 in the English text). It showed a room in a palace; Corneille had stated seventeen years earlier that his countrymen did not feel it suitable for royal personages to speak their inmost thoughts in the open street like Oedipus or Electra, so the feeling of light and free air which is so strong in the text may have been left without visual support—as it was by Jean-Louis Barrault's in many other ways memorable production.[2] The architecture would have been contemporary in style (neo-classic verging on baroque), and as rich in marble and gold as the painted 'flats' could suggest. The actresses' costumes would have been contemporary in style also, and stiff with jewels; while the male actors appear (though the illustrations we can turn to are quite unreliable) to have affected a mixture of the contemporary with a conventionalized version of the Roman emperor garb which is familiar to us all in the 'historical' painting and portrait sculpture of the period (military kilt, cuirass, cloak, and crested helmet).

In an age too early to know the doubtful blessings (in this context) of historical sense and historical realism, contemporary modes cannot have carried any strong suggestion of anachronism. It sufficed to add touches suggestive of majesty and remoteness. Today there are not two periods in contrast —ancient and modern—but three, our own being the third. The urge to dress tragedy in so-called authentic classical costume has come and, on the whole, gone again. The best solution today seems to be the poeticized versions of the original frontispieces of the plays, as we can see them on the modern Paris stage—drawn much rather towards the French seventeenth century in which Racine lived than towards

Greek statues or vase-paintings, which belong to an entirely
different art and tend to make nonsense of his text.

The style of acting required depends on the art of finding
dignified poses, and harmonious groupings, and avoiding all
outward violence. Be it noted that all figures in historical paint-
ings of the time observe the foot-positions of ballet. Racine's
characters do not touch one another (whatever we may see at
the Comédie Française), neither do they run, nor slouch, nor
writhe. Presumably they bow or curtsy; but if ever they sit,
it merits a stage-direction.

The style of speech does not really pose the problems one
would think from watching professional French actors. They,
poor things, have seen too many styles one after the other and
now all together—the conservatoire, the prosaic, the completely anaesthetized. (And the professional producer, in any
country, is no friend of poetry: it competes.) My own convic-
tion—based on amateur student productions which, however
faulty, have at times given me intense satisfaction in this particular—is that Racine's verse will carry any actor through if
only he has a good voice, enough intelligence to understand
what he has to say, and enough humility to wish to add
nothing of his own—certainly not to add emotion, or 'tears in
the voice'. The emotion is all there, in the verse, waiting to
receive simple and respectful utterance. The music is all there,
and must be neither exaggerated nor ignored.

In declamation as in costume, modern taste demands something simpler—and purer perhaps—than Racine's contemporaries. His theatre had what seems to have been a studied,
melodious, but stilted and florid diction; Molière made fun of
it in the name of naturalness. Yet Racine is known to have
coached his star actresses himself; his own ideal, according
to one late tradition, lay midway between the extremes of
prosaism and artificiality.

A word on his metre may be welcome to some readers (to
the rest, I apologize).

The first point to be made concerns French prosody in
general (as it was, up to the 'free verse' and other licences of
the late nineteenth century). Contrary to what happens in
Germanic and other Romance languages, in a line of French
verse the fixed element is the number of syllables, the variable
element is the number of stresses. Stresses are not unalterably

attached to particular syllables of particular words, as in English, Latin or German: what produces a stress is a pause, terminating a breath-group, which ends (always, in theory) on a stress; a marked pause will create a marked stress. If however—this is a detail, but an important one—the stressed word ends with a neutral or so-called 'mute' *e*, the stress falls on the fully-sounded syllable before it; these e's cannot be stressed, but are always counted, and heard (or at least felt) unless elided or at the end of a line; in the latter case the rhyme is called 'feminine', and every alternate couplet, where rhyme goes in couplets, must be of this nature.

The verse of the seventeenth-century drama is the alexandrine, a line of twelve syllables, rhymed in couplets. It was subject at that time to fairly strict rules which nevertheless, in Racine's virtuoso hands, permit of considerable flexibility; no two successive lines of his, unless by intention, have exactly the same rhythm, and he knows how to make this rhythm always arise from and reinforce his meaning. Normally (but norms exist as a framework for variation), normally there is a complete sentence-close—and hence a heavy stress—at the end of each couplet, a strong pause at the end of each line, a fairly strong pause after the sixth syllable of each, and one more pause somewhere in each half-line, more likely near the beginning than the end—but there may be more than one, and there may be none. The *normal* line—which is not all that common—thus has the rhythm (but much less heavily and less regularly stressed) of *Bonnie Dundee*, or

The Assyrian came down like the wolf on the fold;

never the iambic rhythm of the English 'Alexandrine':

Our sweetest songs are those that tell of saddest thought.

Normal is the line:

Tout m'affli/ge‿et me nuit,// et conspi/re‿à me nuire//

But the heaviest pause in a line may come in any of the intermediate places mentioned; while, rarely, the sixth or twelfth syllable may be run over by the sense ('enjambement'), with the effect of isolating the overflow (*le rejet*) between the pause the ear expected and the delayed pause which it hears:

Mais tout n'est pas détruit; // Et vous en laissez vivre⏝
Un . . .

Or the heavy pause may precede the pause which we expected to be the stronger of the two, producing a *contre-rejet*:

Où me cacher ?// *Fuyons*/ dans la nuit/ infernale.//
Mais que dis//-je ? *Mon père*/ y tient l'ur/ne fatale.//

The total effect, like that of fine dancing, is an illusion of perfect freedom:

Oui, Prin//ce, je languis,/ je brû//le pour Thésée./
Je l'ai//me, non point tel/ que l'ont vu/ les Enfers,/
Volage adorateur/ de mille objets/ divers,/
Qui va/ du Dieu des Morts/ déshonorer/ la couche,/
Mais fidè//le, mais fier,// et mê/me⏝un peu farouche,/
Charmant,// jeu//ne, traînant/ tous les cœurs après soi,/
Tel/ qu'on dépeint/ nos Dieux,// ou tel/ que je vous voi.//

But the great secret of Racine is not even here, but in the music
of his words, which it would take a technical analysis to demon-
strate. To the trained ear, this is perhaps the sweetest music in
all poetry.

None of all this, unfortunately, can come through in translation.[3] Translations are made because it is desirable that the
English-reading public should have some idea what the name
of Racine stands for; but the ideal of the translator—that anything a reasonable critic could say of the original could be said
of his work, and *vice versa*—is more obviously unrealizable
here than with many other authors. There might be some hope
if we could find an English poet equal to Racine and similar in
his taste; but the chance is slender, and such a man might
prefer to do other things with his time.

Contemporary England never knew Racine because its
writers never represented him adequately in English.[4] They
failed presumably because they did not care for the merits of
his drama, too discreet for them in its effects, but at the same
time too honest in its treatment of character and passion. Our
seventeenth century recognized the same hierarchy of genres
as the French, with tragedy very high, but below epic and
ode: but we sought elevation in 'the frequent use of bold and
daring figures' and epithets;[5] Racine's age sought it mainly by

excluding 'low' words and expressions (and the low often meant the concrete and particular),[6] and by banning all that could startle and disconcert, in the name of clarity, or dramatic verisimilitude, or good taste; in the last analysis, in the name of good breeding.

Now these two exclusions are unheard-of in English poetry. It is from the inferiority of its images, alone, that Dr F.R. Leavis has pronounced Dryden's *All for Love* to be poetically, and even dramatically, unworthy to be put in the same class with *Antony and Cleopatra*.[7] Whereas French taste after the middle of the seventeenth century was happy only with figures of rhetoric that were utterly familiar, clichés that are a real obstacle to the modern reader (English or French) but which obviously still held magic then. I mean principally those stock images of love as a sickness, love as a wound, as a fire, as torture, as defeat, as enslavement; we had them all, though less obsessively no doubt, in the lyrics of our own poets from the Restoration to the Romantics: 'Love is itself its own sickness and pain . . . Thou canst not raise forces enough to rebel . . .' These were in fact the form then acceptable of that heightening of style we call poetic diction; for, as Gilbert Murray once pointed out, poetic diction includes not only or mainly 'those expressions unknown to common life' used, so says Aristotle in the *Poetics*, to 'save the language from commonness', but also expressions handed down from poets of old, which produce by long association 'the expectation of poetry' in the hearer or reader.[8] In much the same way, it has been argued, when Racine's public went to the theatre, the *palais à volonté*, which they knew already, helped to attune their minds to tragedy, precisely because of the other tragedies for which they had seen it used.[9]

Otway's *Titus and Berenice*, adapted from Racine's *Bérénice*, simply shows the distance between French and English taste at the time. The manner of *Bérénice* is plainer than that of *Phèdre*; Otway evidently saw no merit in Racine's studied avoidance of heroics in sentiment or style, and seems not to have grasped the subtleties of expression and intention that give it its great poetic value. Just as he has tampered with the plot and spoilt it, he has pruned, hacked and embellished the text, until there is not a speech of a dozen lines remaining that could be quoted against a parallel in French.

Dryden, on the other hand, did once revise a Shakespearean tragedy in a way which Racine conceivably might have approved. *All for Love*, decried by Mr Leavis, takes out of the sprawling action of *Antony and Cleopatra* what will fit into the last day of the hero's and heroine's lives, observing the unities, as the poet observes, 'more exactly . . . than perhaps the English theatre requires.' The action can no longer show the return of Antony from Egypt, his reconciliation with Octavian, his relapse, then Actium, then the last fight and the suicides: it becomes the spectacle of attempts by friends and followers to wean Antony from the queen while Caesar is at the gates of Alexandria. Two engagements take place off-stage (though Antony fights only in the first), Cleopatra's 'monument' is abolished, and decorum censors all mention of Antony's drinking habits (*a fortiori* the 'eight wild boars roasted whole at a breakfast, and but twelve persons there', II ii). In style, Dryden announces that he has 'professed to imitate the divine Shakespeare', and he abandons rhyme. In fact he often suggests Racine—echoes him indeed from time to time. It still seems to be *Bérénice* that is in his mind most often.

His characters watch each other's expressions as Racine's do (and Otway's do not):

> Now, what news, my Charmion?
> Will he be kind? and will he not forsake me?
> Am I to live, or die?—nay, do I live?
> Or am I dead? for when he gave his answer,
> Fate took the word, and then I lived or died.
> *Charmion.* I found him, madam—
> *Cleopatra.*   A long speech preparing?
> If thou bringst comfort, haste, and give it me,
> For never was more need.
> *Iras.*   I know he loves you.
> *Cleopatra.* Had he been kind, her eyes had told me so,
> Before her tongue could speak it: Now she studies
> To soften what he said . . .

> *Antony.* Well, madam, we are met.
> *Cleopatra.*   Is this a meeting?
> Then, we must part?
> *Antony.*   We must.

Cleopatra.   Who says we must?
Antony.   Our own hard fates.
Cleopatra.   We made those fates ourselves . . .

Antony.   How I loved.
Witness, ye days and nights, and all ye hours,
That danced away with down upon your feet
As all your business were to count my passion!
One day passed by, and nothing saw but love;
Another came, and still 'twas only love;
The suns were wearied out with looking on,
And I untired with loving.
I saw you every day, and all the day;
And every day was still but as the first,
So eager was I still to see you more.   (Act II)

But these impressions do not last: Dryden still uses those con-
spicuous concrete images which all English poetry has relied
on:

Oh, she has decked his ruin with her love,
Led him in golden bands to gaudy slaughter,
And made perdition pleasing: she has left him
The blank of what he was.   (Act I)

And he still runs a little too much to fustian:

Come on, my soldier!
Our hearts and arms are still the same: I long
Once more to meet our foes; that thou and I
Like Time and Death, marching before our troops,
May taste fate to them; mow them out a passage,
And, entering where the foremost squadrons yield,
Begin the noble harvest of the field.   (Ibid.)

We find nothing of *Phèdre* in *All for Love*, for the two plays
(and *Titus and Berenice* makes a third) came out in the same
year, 1677. Dryden's preface contains a reference to *Phèdre* so
hostile that it suggests more interest than he cared to admit (it
concerned the Frenchified scrupulousness of 'Monsieur
Hippolyte'); but no other play of his leans so far towards
Racine.

Phèdre was adapted for the London stage once, in 1707, by
Edmund Smith, with a garbled plot, a florid style and a happy

ending (for the virtuous lovers), to considerable contemporary acclaim.

After 1723 no more acting versions of Racine were made in English until our own time, though published translations of single plays have succeeded one another ever since, in tune with almost every shift of poetic taste.

The worthy but wooden R. B. Boswell (1889)—until very lately the only verse-translator of the complete dramatic works[10]—wrote with no view to stage performance; with no view at all, indeed, except to produce a faithful rendering in an easy and rather shambling form of blank verse, with *enjambements* wherever it suited him to make them.

Only one English poet of some standing has attempted to translate Racine, and this was in our own century. (The word translate I use of course in the sense defined above, which is the opposite of what has lately been done in America by Mr Robert Lowell.) The poet seems on the face of it one of the least likely to succeed: it was John Masefield.[11] But, at least in patches, he did succeed. At least he gives an idea of Racine, grave, simple, tender (it is *Bérénice* once more), and he gives pleasure.

> I loved her, she loved me; and since that day—
> I cannot say if it were glad or sorry—
> Her life has had no object but her love.
> Unknown at Court, a stranger here in Rome,
> She passes all her days with no more thought
> Save that she see me some time, and the rest
> Expect to see me.
> And if, as sometimes happens, I am late,
> I find her weeping.
> All that there is most powerful in love—
> Joy, beauty, glory, virtue, are in her.
> For five long years each day that I have seen her
> Has given me the joy the first sight had.

If however we compare this with the original, we find that he has taken the liberties of an equal. The four lines before the final sentence quoted represent eight in the French, which has been crushed like a handful of snow—yet, in this case, with little lost. The play as a whole has been compressed and cut with less success.

Of translators who now hold the field, it would ill become me to speak critically about those (J. Cairncross, K. Muir, S. Solomon) whose style and methods are close to those I have tried to use. Of Professor Lacy Lockert I will only note that he leans harder than I think desirable on a synthetic archaism of diction.

Perhaps I may venture to break a lance against the collective entity I think of as the Penguin Classics. Some of the team originally gathered by Dr E. V. Rieu desert blank verse for stranger and what seem to me uncouther metres, some often prefer prose; nearly all are courageously and unrelentingly modern. Some seem so anxious to spare the reader all sense of strangeness that they dare not credit him with any literary culture at all. Thus, 'thou' is banned from the *Penguin Book of French Verse* even in translating Christian poems addressed to God (the modern reader does not say his prayers). Thus again, Mr P. Vellacott asserts 'Modern English does not say "Touch not", but "Do not touch"'.[12] (He is defending a prose scene of his *Hippolytus* against Gilbert Murray's over-decorated verse translation; like others of his team he seems to shun the Scylla of Wardour Street more zealously than the Charybdis of Fleet Street.)

I would submit that there is a zone, which I should call that of literary tradition, between everyday speech and the frankly archaic, and as a translator of Racine I feel the need to draw on it. It will be needed, with all other kinds of compromise, if the difficulties of the task are to be evaded (not surmounted, for to surmount them is impossible). The clichés cannot be eliminated, but can be thinned out. Some of the abstractions can be made concrete in accordance with the real sense.

The hierarchical conception of style is an obstacle. Semanticists nowadays know more about it than poets. It did not of course mean that Racine had only one tone at his disposal: he had a fairly broad waveband, with a sharp lower edge, but within which impressive variety was possible. Only, it is necessary to have some notion of its limits to appreciate its variations. The higher flights may not be harder to cope with than that very simple diction which seems at times to fall below the limits altogether. 'Ne verrez-vous point Phèdre avant que de partir, Seigneur ?'

Perhaps the ability to understand, and to feel, all the poet's intentions, with dignity, and simplicity wherever Racine is simple, are nearly enough in a translator. But there must be one thing more: the power to move. I doubt if emotion often comes through the laboured diction of, for instance, Boswell. I do not think we can leave it to situation and plot to take control and produce their own effects: to this extent at least we must all agree with the critics who say that Racine sacrificed the mechanics of drama to higher values.

But by what exactly is the tragic emotion achieved? By subtle and imaginative 'psychology', said nineteenth-century critics. By the contrast between the greatness of situations and the simplicity of tone, says M. Thierry Maulnier. Much more, in the last resort, by something I have hardly mentioned— sheer verbal melody. It is a point that it is tactless to mention to a translator: it goes without saying that he will bear it in mind, and it goes without saying that he cannot be expected to do very much about it, having so much else on his hands, and cannot fairly be blamed if he fails you at the critical point.

But if he fails there, he has failed, with Racine, utterly. He must look on the music as one of the essentials, even though his efforts will never produce anything so exact as a transposition.

In the version printed here, which is already more than twenty years old, the solace of wartime leisures, I had some of these ideas in mind, and decided to adopt the following principles (which are added here in explanation, not excuse).

I chose blank verse as my metre, since it has had in English the same pre-eminence and the same functions as the alexandrine in France, and comes to our hands laden with associations and resonances ('the expectation of poetry'), flexible and resourceful after centuries of experiment. I know that some modern poets have expressed themselves as being tired of it: I suspect most readers are not. It should carry some reminders of the greater strictness of Racine's rhymed metre; no half-lines, for instance, and *enjambements* as seldom as possible unless justified by the rhythm of the original.

The vocabulary should be that of today, but of the *literature* of today; selective, rejecting journalese, slang and the blurred speech of lazy minds. It must preserve the air of breeding in Racine's characters. It would have to be wider than his, for our terms have not been forced by scarcity into the same wealth of connotations. It should not be archaic, or should contain nothing so archaic that, in its context, it would make a modern actor uncomfortable: but also no turns of speech that would strike a modern as being modern. It should have as little recourse as possible to paraphrase or excision: Racine's lovers' jargon, in which nothing is without its analogue somewhere in our literature, should be sometimes retained, so that this coloration of the poetry should be present, but not more obtrusive than we may think it was in seventeenth-century Paris.

My one wish is that this *Phaedra* should take a place with the other attempts now being made, however belatedly, to show the reading public (or perhaps the theatre public) of English-speaking countries what poetry and what tragic drama there is in Racine. All strong literary influences today are international, and it is hard to think that there can be real incompatibilities to keep us from him for ever.

A word must be added about the proper names in the play, since such chaos reigns today about all words of classical origin in English. A whole generation has been taught to pronounce the ancient tongues approximately as we think the ancients did: but the names of history and legend came to us through French and English and suffered the sound-changes of both—became in fact English words. A few such very familiar cases remain unchallenged: the *c* changed from *k* to *s* in Cerberus, Thucydides (Greek) as in Caesar, Cicero (Latin); the vowels in Aphrodite, Plato, as in Caesar (again) or Cato. Racine received his Greek names with not only the sound-values gallicized but the endings too; and there can be no doubt that this helped him to make French poetry with them.

Since, then, this translation has been made with the traditional spellings, and with the traditional English sound-values in mind, I hope it will be read as it was written—and, especially, that it will be spoken so if it is ever performed. I have appended a glossary of pronunciations; the stresses are of course even more important (for metre) than the vowels and consonants.

One word forms a slight exception to these principles. For the place-name appearing in *Phèdre* as *Trézène* the regular English equivalent would be *Troezen*—which would have to be pronounced like 'treason', and would create confusion.

Happily Gilbert Murray's Oxford text of Euripides adopts a spelling which replaces the diphthong with a simple *o*, and I have seized on this more convenient form. It is written *Trozén* and rhymes with 'queen' in Murray's translation; it could be *Trozĕn*, on the analogy of 'amen'; but the shift of stress and lengthened vowel that I have given it (*Trózen*) have an exact analogy, I believe, in the name Plato.

The French text is reproduced, with permission, from my critical edition for the Manchester University Press (1943). It is that of the *Œuvres de Racine* of 1697, the last published in the poet's lifetime; the play has very few variants.

The punctuation is of that edition, except for the omission of certain obtrusive commas not present in earlier editions. Several capital letters, absent in other modern texts, have been preserved as helpful indications of emphasis or solemnity of tone.

NOTES

1. Cf. Winifred Newton, *Le thème de Phèdre et d'Hippolyte dans la littérature française*, Droz, 1939; J. Pommier, *Aspects de Racine*, Nizet, 1954, pp. 363 ff.
2. See his ed. of *Phèdre*, Seuil, 1946.
3. Much of what follows is adapted, with permission, from my article 'On translating Racine' in *Studies in Modern French Literature presented to P. Mansell Jones*, Manchester, 1961, pp. 181–95.
4. Cf. Katherine E. Wheatley, *Racine and English Classicism*. University of Texas Press, 1956.
5. Congreve, cit. Wheatley, op. cit., p. 227.
6. Cf. J. G. Cahen, *Le vocabulaire de Racine*, Droz, 1946.
7. '"Antony and Cleopatra" and "All for Love"', *Scrutiny* v (1937), pp. 158 ff.
8. *The Classical Tradition in Poetry*, Oxford, 1927, pp. 125–6.
9. A. Beijer, 'Le théâtre de Charles XII et la mise en scène du théâtre parlé au XVIIe Siècle', *Revue d'Histoire du Théâtre*, 1956, p. 213.
10. In Bohn's Standard Library.
11. *Bérénice* and (less strikingly successful) *Esther*, pub. separately, Heinemann, 1922.
12. Euripides, *The Bacchae and Other Plays*, Penguin Classics, 1954, p. 33.

Further Reading

G. Lytton Strachey, *Racine* (dated 1908), in *Literary Essays* (*Collected Works*, Chatto & Windus, 1948, pp. 58 ff.)

E. Vinaver (trs. P. Mansell Jones), *Racine and poetic Tragedy*. Manchester, 1955.

J. C. Lapp, *Aspects of Racinian Tragedy*. Toronto and Oxford, 1955, 1964.

P. France, *Racine's Rhetoric*. Oxford, 1965.

O. de Mourgues, *Racine, or The Triumph of Relevance*. Cambridge, 1967.

R. C. Knight, *Racine* [14 critical essays in English] ('Modern Judgements'). Macmillan, 1969.

PHÈDRE
Tragédie

PRÉFACE

Voici encore une tragédie dont le sujet est pris d'Euripide. Quoique j'aie suivi une route un peu différente de celle de cet auteur pour la conduite de l'action, je n'ai pas laissé d'enrichir ma pièce de tout ce qui m'a paru plus éclatant dans la sienne. Quand je ne lui devrais que la seule idée du caractère de Phèdre, je pourrais dire que je lui dois ce que j'ai peut-être mis de plus raisonnable sur le théâtre. Je ne suis point étonné que ce caractère ait eu un succès si heureux du temps d'Euripide, et qu'il ait encore si bien réussi dans notre siècle, puisqu'il a toutes les qualités qu'Aristote demande dans le héros de la tragédie, et qui sont propres à exciter la compassion et la terreur. En effet, Phèdre n'est ni tout à fait coupable, ni tout à fait innocente. Elle est engagée par sa destinée, et par la colère des Dieux, dans une passion illégitime dont elle a horreur toute la première. Elle fait tous ses efforts pour la surmonter. Elle aime mieux se laisser mourir, que de la déclarer à personne. Et lorsqu'elle est forcée de la découvrir, elle en parle avec une confusion, qui fait bien voir que son crime est plutôt une punition des Dieux, qu'un mouvement de sa volonté.

J'ai même pris soin de la rendre un peu moins odieuse qu'elle n'est dans les tragédies des anciens, où elle se résout d'elle-même à accuser Hippolyte. J'ai cru que la calomnie avait quelque chose de trop bas et de trop noir pour la mettre dans la bouche d'une Princesse, qui a d'ailleurs des sentiments si nobles et si vertueux. Cette bassesse m'a paru plus convenable à une nourrice, qui pouvait avoir des inclinations plus serviles, et qui néanmoins n'entreprend cette fausse accusation que pour sauver la vie et l'honneur de sa maîtresse. Phèdre n'y donne les mains que parce qu'elle est dans une agitation d'esprit qui la met hors d'elle-même, et elle vient un moment après dans le dessein de justifier l'innocence, et de déclarer la vérité.

Hippolyte est accusé dans Euripide et dans Sénèque d'avoir en effet violé sa belle-mère. *Vim corpus tulit*. Mais il n'est ici

PREFACE

Here is another tragedy on a subject taken from Euripides. The action follows a somewhat different course, but I have enriched my play with everything in his that I considered most strikingly beautiful. Had I borrowed no more than the conception of Phaedra's character, I might say I owe him the most reasonable thing, perhaps, that I have given to the theatre. I am not surprised that this character was so successful in Euripides' time, and now again in our own, considering that it has every quality required by Aristotle in the tragic hero, and proper to arouse compassion and terror. For Phaedra is not altogether guilty, and not altogether innocent. She is drawn by her destiny, and the anger of the Gods, into an unlawful passion which she is the first to hold in horror. She makes every endeavour to overcome it. She chooses death rather than disclose it to anyone. And when forced to reveal it, she speaks of it with such shame and confusion as leave no doubt that her crime is rather a punishment from the Gods, than an impulse of her own will.

I have even taken pains to make her a little less odious than she is in the tragedies of antiquity, where she brings herself, unprompted, to accuse Hippolytus. I felt that a false testimony was something too base, too black, to put into the mouth of a Princess possessed otherwise of sentiments so noble and virtuous. Such baseness seemed to me more fitting to a Nurse, who might have more slave-like propensities; though even she only enters upon the lying accusation to save the life and honour of her mistress. If Phaedra acquiesces, it is because she is beside herself in the agitation of her thoughts, and the next moment she comes on with the intention of vindicating the guiltless and publishing the truth.

Hippolytus is accused, in Euripides and in Seneca, of actually violating his step-mother—*vim corpus tulit*; here, of no more than the intention. I desired to spare Theseus a sense of outrage which might have made him less acceptable to my audience.

accusé que d'en avoir eu le dessein. J'ai voulu épargner à Thésée une confusion qui l'aurait pu rendre moins agréable aux spectateurs.

Pour ce qui est du personnage d'Hippolyte, j'avais remarqué dans les Anciens, qu'on reprochait à Euripide de l'avoir représenté comme un philosophe exempt de toute imperfection. Ce qui faisait que la mort de ce jeune Prince causait beaucoup plus d'indignation que de pitié. J'ai cru lui devoir donner quelque faiblesse qui le rendrait un peu coupable envers son père, sans pourtant lui rien ôter de cette grandeur d'âme avec laquelle il épargne l'honneur de Phèdre, et se laisse opprimer sans l'accuser. J'appelle faiblesse la passion qu'il ressent malgré lui pour Aricie, qui est la fille et la sœur des ennemis mortels de son père.

Cette Aricie n'est point un personnage de mon invention. Virgile dit qu'Hippolyte l'épousa et en eut un fils après qu'Esculape l'eut ressuscité. Et j'ai lu encore dans quelques auteurs qu'Hippolyte avait épousé et emmené en Italie une jeune Athénienne de grande naissance, qui s'appelait Aricie, et qui avait donné son nom à une petite ville d'Italie.

Je rapporte ces autorités, parce que je me suis très scrupuleusement attaché à suivre la Fable. J'ai même suivi l'histoire de Thésée telle qu'elle est dans Plutarque.

C'est dans cet historien que j'ai trouvé que ce qui avait donné occasion de croire que Thésée fût descendu dans les Enfers pour enlever Proserpine, était un voyage que ce Prince avait fait en Épire vers la source de l'Achéron, chez un Roi dont Pirithoüs voulait enlever la femme, et qui arrêta Thésée prisonnier après avoir fait mourir Pirithoüs. Ainsi j'ai tâché de conserver la vraisemblance de l'histoire, sans rien perdre des ornements de la Fable qui fournit extrêmement à la Poésie. Et le bruit de la mort de Thésée fondé sur ce voyage fabuleux, donne lieu à Phèdre de faire une déclaration d'amour, qui devient une des principales causes de son malheur, et qu'elle n'aurait jamais osé faire tant qu'elle aurait cru que son mari était vivant.

Au reste, je n'ose encore assurer que cette pièce soit en effet la meilleure de mes tragédies. Je laisse et aux lecteurs et au temps à décider de son véritable prix. Ce que je puis assurer, c'est que je n'en ai point fait où la vertu soit plus mise en jour que dans celle-ci. Les moindres fautes y sont sévèrement

As for the figure of Hippolytus, I had read in ancient authors that Euripides was blamed for depicting him as a philosopher free of all imperfection—so that the death of the youthful Prince gave rise to far more indignation than pity. I felt I should give him a failing that might render him somewhat guilty towards his father, without detracting at all from that magnanimity which makes him spare Phaedra's honour and go to his doom without accusing her. By failing I mean his involuntary passion for Aricia, the daughter and the sister of his father's mortal enemies.

This Aricia is not a child of my invention. Vergil relates that Hippolytus married her, and she bore him a son, after Aesculapius had brought him back to life. And I have read too, in certain authors, that Hippolytus had married and brought into Italy an Athenian maiden of high birth, named Aricia, who had given her name to an Italian township.

I adduce these authorities, because I have most scrupulously endeavoured to keep close to the legend. I have even taken the history of Theseus just as it is in Plutarch.

It is this historian who mentions that the belief in Theseus' descent to the underworld to abduct Proserpine, was occasioned by a journey he made into Epirus towards the source of the Acheron, where a King, whose wife Pirithous sought to carry off, held Theseus prisoner after putting Pirithous to death. Thus I have tried to retain the verisimilitude of history, and yet to lose none of the embellishments of fable, so rich in the stuff of poetry. And the rumour of Theseus' death, based on the legendary journey, gives rise to that declaration of Phaedra's love which proves one of the principal causes of her unhappy plight, and which she would never have dared utter while she believed her husband to be alive.

For the rest, I dare not yet assert this play to be in truth the best of my tragedies. I leave my readers, and time, to set its rightful price upon it. What I can assert is that I have composed none where virtue is shown to more advantage than here. The slightest faults are severely punished. The bare thought of crime is regarded with no less horror than crime itself. The failings of love are treated as real failings. The passions are offered to view only to show all the ravage they create. And vice is everywhere painted in such hues, that its hideous face may be recognized and loathed. Here is the proper aim for

punies. La seule pensée du crime y est regardée avec autant d'horreur que le crime même. Les faiblesses de l'amour y passent pour de vraies faiblesses. Les passions n'y sont présentées aux yeux que pour montrer tout le désordre dont elles sont cause : Et le vice y est peint partout avec des couleurs qui en font connaître et haïr la difformité. C'est là proprement le but que tout homme qui travaille pour le public doit se proposer. Et c'est ce que les premiers poètes tragiques avaient en vue sur toute chose. Leur théâtre était une école où la vertu n'était pas moins bien enseignée que dans les écoles des philosophes. Aussi Aristote a bien voulu donner des règles du poème dramatique ; et Socrate, le plus sage des philosophes, ne dédaignait pas de mettre la main aux tragédies d'Euripide. Il serait à souhaiter que nos ouvrages fussent aussi solides et aussi pleins d'utiles instructions que ceux de ces poètes. Ce serait peut-être un moyen de réconcilier la tragédie avec quantité de personnes célèbres par leur piété et par leur doctrine, qui l'ont condamnée dans ces derniers temps, et qui en jugeraient sans doute plus favorablement, si les auteurs songeaient autant à instruire leurs spectateurs qu'à les divertir, et s'ils suivaient en cela la véritable intention de la tragédie.

every man to keep in sight who works for the public. And this, above all, was the purpose of the earliest tragic poets. Their stage was a school where virtue was taught no less well than in the schools of the philosophers. Thus Aristotle consented to draw up rules for the dramatic poem; Socrates, the sagest of the philosophers, thought it no shame to set his hand to the tragedies of Euripides. It were much to be desired that our works should be found as serious and as full of useful instruction as the pages of those poets. It might bring about a reconciliation between the tragic art and a number of persons, noted for their religion and learning, who have denounced it of late, but might well look upon it with less disfavour if authors cared as much to instruct as to entertain their audience, and carried out thereby the true purpose of tragedy.

ACTEURS

THÉSÉE, fils d'Égée, Roi d'Athènes.

PHÈDRE, femme de Thésée, fille de Minos et de Pasiphaé.

HIPPOLYTE, fils de Thésée, et d'Antiope Reine des Amazones.

ARICIE, Princesse du sang royal d'Athènes.

ŒNONE, nourrice et confidente de Phèdre.

THÉRAMÈNE, gouverneur d'Hippolyte.

ISMÈNE, confidente d'Aricie.

PANOPE, femme de la suite de Phèdre.

GARDES

La scène est à Trézène, ville du Péloponnèse.

DRAMATIS PERSONAE

THESEUS, son of Aegeus, King of Athens.

PHAEDRA, wife of Theseus, and daughter of King Minos
of Crete and Pasiphaë.

HIPPOLYTUS, son of Theseus by Antiope Queen of the
Amazons.

ARÍCIA, daughter of Pallas, descended from the ancient
Kings of Athens.

OENONE, formerly Nurse of Phaedra.

THERÁMENES, preceptor and attendant to Hippolytus.

ISMÉNE, confidant of Aricia.

PÁNOPE, one of Phaedra's women.

GUARDS

*The scene is in the royal residence at Trozen, a dependency of
Athens in the Peloponnese.*

Acte Premier

HIPPOLYTE

Le dessein en est pris, je pars, cher Théramène,
Et quitte le séjour de l'aimable Trézène.
Dans le doute mortel dont je suis agité
Je commence à rougir de mon oisiveté.
Depuis plus de six mois éloigné de mon père
J'ignore le destin d'une tête si chère.
J'ignore jusqu'aux lieux qui le peuvent cacher.

THÉRAMÈNE

Et dans quels lieux, Seigneur, l'allez-vous donc chercher?
Déjà pour satisfaire à votre juste crainte,
10 J'ai couru les deux mers que sépare Corinthe.
J'ai demandé Thésée aux peuples de ces bords
Où l'on voit l'Achéron se perdre chez les morts.
J'ai visité l'Elide, et laissant le Ténare,
Passé jusqu'à la mer, qui vit tomber Icare.
Sur quel espoir nouveau, dans quels heureux climats
Croyez-vous découvrir la trace de ses pas?
Qui sait même, qui sait si le Roi votre père
Veut que de son absence on sache le mystère?
Et si lorsqu'avec vous nous tremblons pour ses jours,
20 Tranquille, et nous cachant de nouvelles amours
Ce héros n'attend point qu'une amante abusée ...

HIPPOLYTE

Cher Théramène, arrête, et respecte Thésée.
De ses jeunes erreurs désormais revenu
Par un indigne obstacle il n'est point retenu;
Et fixant de ses vœux l'inconstance fatale
Phèdre depuis longtemps ne craint plus de rivale.

Act One

HIPPOLYTUS

I have made up my mind, Theramenes.
No more for me the tranquil days of Trozen,
For in the mortal tempest of my doubts
I am dishonoured if I linger here.
Six months ago my father sailed and left me
Ignorant what befalls a head so cherished,
Ignorant even where he may be hidden—

THERAMENES

So where will you go to look for him, my lord?
Already, to relieve a fear I shared,

10 I have scoured the two seas that Corinth holds asunder,
Demanded Theseus of the tribes that live
Where Acheron drives down headlong into Hell,
Searched Elis, skirted Taenarum, and even
Traversed the waves where Icarus fell and perished.
What hope new-risen or what happier skies
Will light you to his footsteps? Why, perhaps,
Who knows, perhaps the King your father wishes
Not to unveil the mystery of his venture,
And while his peril fills your thought and ours,

20 Serene, weaving the latest of his loves,
The hero waits to seize the unguarded moment—

HIPPOLYTUS

Stop, good Theramenes. You slander Theseus;
There is a nobler cause for these delays;
After the follies of forgotten youth
The wanderings of his inconstant heart
Are fixed at length, and Phaedra fears no rival.

Enfin en le cherchant je suivrai mon devoir,
Et je fuirai ces lieux que je n'ose plus voir.

THÉRAMÈNE

Hé depuis quand, Seigneur, craignez-vous la présence
30 De ces paisibles lieux, si chers à votre enfance,
Et dont je vous ai vu préférer le séjour
Au tumulte pompeux d'Athène et de la Cour ?
Quel péril, ou plutôt quel chagrin vous en chasse ?

HIPPOLYTE

Cet heureux temps n'est plus. Tout a changé de face
Depuis que sur ces bords les Dieux ont envoyé
La fille de Minos et de Pasiphaé.

THÉRAMÈNE

J'entends. De vos douleurs la cause m'est connue,
Phèdre ici vous chagrine, et blesse votre vue.
Dangereuse marâtre, à peine elle vous vit,
40 Que votre exil d'abord signala son crédit.
Mais sa haine sur vous autrefois attachée
Ou s'est évanouie, ou s'est bien relâchée.
Et d'ailleurs quels périls vous peut faire courir
Une femme mourante, et qui cherche à mourir ?
Phèdre atteinte d'un mal qu'elle s'obstine à taire,
Lasse enfin d'elle-même, et du jour qui l'éclaire,
Peut-elle contre vous former quelques desseins ?

HIPPOLYTE

Sa vaine inimitié n'est pas ce que je crains.
Hippolyte en partant fuit une autre ennemie.
50 Je fuis, je l'avoûrai, cette jeune Aricie
Reste d'un sang fatal conjuré contre nous.

THÉRAMÈNE

Quoi ! vous-même, Seigneur, la persécutez-vous ?
Jamais l'aimable sœur des cruels Pallantides
Trempa-t-elle aux complots de ses frères perfides ?
Et devez-vous haïr ses innocents appas ?

HIPPOLYTE

Si je la haïssais, je ne la fuirais pas.

THÉRAMÈNE

Seigneur, m'est-il permis d'expliquer votre fuite ?

So once more—I shall go where duty points
And leave a land I cannot bear to see.

THERAMENES

But my lord, how long have you despised the presence
30 Of these calm fields, the pleasure of your childhood
Whose solitude was dearer to you than
The splendid stir of Athens and the Court?
What fear has banished you, or else what heartache?

HIPPOLYTUS

Those days are past. Pleasure and peace have vanished
Since first the Gods directed to our shore
The child of Minos and Pasiphaë.

THERAMENES

I see: there is the cause, the hated presence—
Phaedra, who came, your father's dangerous bride,
Looked on you once, and by your prompt exile
40 Gave the first measure of her new-won power.
But all that dogged hate and old aversion
Has passed with time, passed or at least abated;
And after all what danger lies in her,
A woman dying, crying out for death?
Stricken by ills that none can make her utter,
Tired of her life, tired of the day that lights her
What can she do to you?

HIPPOLYTUS

                I do not fear
Anything her aversion could devise.
I go to escape another enemy,
50 I do admit: I fly Aricia,
The youngest and the last of all that house
In fatal league against ours.

THERAMENES

                You, my lord,
Are turned against her too? But Pallas' daughter
Surely had no part in her brothers' treason,
And must you hate that unoffending grace?

HIPPOLYTUS

I'd not avoid her if I hated her.

THERAMENES

My lord, have I permission to interpret
Your leaving? Must I think that you are not

Pourriez-vous n'être plus ce superbe Hippolyte,
Implacable ennemi des amoureuses lois,
60 Et d'un joug que Thésée a subi tant de fois ?
Vénus par votre orgueil si longtemps méprisée,
Voudrait-elle à la fin justifier Thésée ?
Et vous mettant au rang du reste des mortels,
Vous a-t-elle forcé d'encenser ses autels ?
Aimeriez-vous, Seigneur ?

HIPPOLYTE

                    Ami, qu'oses-tu dire ?
Toi qui connais mon cœur depuis que je respire,
Des sentiments d'un cœur si fier, si dédaigneux,
Peux-tu me demander le désaveu honteux ?
C'est peu qu'avec son lait une mère amazone
70 M'ait fait sucer encor cet orgueil qui t'étonne.
Dans un âge plus mûr moi-même parvenu
Je me suis applaudi, quand je me suis connu.
Attaché près de moi par un zèle sincère
Tu me contais alors l'histoire de mon père.
Tu sais combien mon âme attentive à ta voix
S'échauffait au récit de ses nobles exploits;
Quand tu me dépeignais ce héros intrépide
Consolant les mortels de l'absence d'Alcide,
Les Monstres étouffés, et les Brigands punis,
80 Procruste, Cercyon, et Scirron, et Sinnis,
Et les os dispersés du Géant d'Épidaure,
Et la Crète fumant du sang du Minotaure.
Mais quand tu récitais des faits moins glorieux,
Sa foi partout offerte, et reçue en cent lieux,
Hélène à ses parents dans Sparte dérobée,
Salamine témoin des pleurs de Péribée,
Tant d'autres, dont les noms lui sont même échappés,
Trop crédules esprits que sa flamme a trompés;
Ariane aux rochers contant ses injustices,
90 Phèdre enlevée enfin sous de meilleurs auspices;
Tu sais comme à regret écoutant ce discours,
Je te pressais souvent d'en abréger le cours:
Heureux ! si j'avais pu ravir à la mémoire
Cette indigne moitié d'une si belle histoire.
Et moi-même à mon tour je me verrais lié ?

The old implacable Hippolytus,
60 The outlaw of Love's empire, he that vowed
Never to wear the yoke his father wore?
Can it be that a slighted and a smarting Goddess
Will press you to the service of her shrine,
Reduce you to the rank of common men
And vindicate that father by your fate?
Can it be love, my lord?

HIPPOLYTUS

       How can you say it,
My friend, that knew the childhood of my heart
And all its growth in pride and fierce resolve?
Shall I dishonour it, disown myself?
70 First, as a babe, at an Amazonian breast
I drank the resolution that astounds you,
But once of age to look upon myself
I wished to be no other than I was.
Then, in the faithful service of your kindness
As you rehearsed for me my father's story,
Do you remember how my soul blazed up
At each particular in the noble toils
Of the intrepid hero, as you showed him
Turning the world from thoughts of lost Alcides
80 By monsters strangled and by brigands slain —
Procrustes, Sinnis, Sciro, Cercyon
And Epidaurus scattered with the limbs
Of her gigantic tyrant, and the gore
Reeking from all Crete, of the Minotaur?
But when you told other ignobler feats—
A faith so cheaply pledged, and ever new,
Helen torn from a mother's arms in Sparta;
In Salamis the sighs of Periboea;
So many more than he can even name,
90 Victims too credulous of a lover's tongue;
What empty shores heard Ariadne's sorrows;
How Phaedra, last and under happier auspice,
Followed him—then I wished the tale untold;
Often I urged you hasten and be done;
And would my wishes had redeemed from fame
That darker half of such a fair renown!
And now, by the spite of Heaven, shall I be

Et les Dieux jusque-là m'auraient humilié ?
Dans mes lâches soupirs d'autant plus méprisable,
Qu'un long amas d'honneurs rend Thésée excusable,
Qu'aucuns Monstres par moi domptés jusqu'aujourd'hui,
100 Ne m'ont acquis le droit de faillir comme lui.
Quand même ma fierté pourrait s'être adoucie,
Aurais-je pour vainqueur dû choisir Aricie ?
Ne souviendrait-il plus à mes sens égarés
De l'obstacle éternel qui nous a séparés ?
Mon père la réprouve, et par des lois sévères
Il défend de donner des neveux à ses frères ;
D'une tige coupable il craint un rejeton.
Il veut avec leur sœur ensevelir leur nom,
Et que jusqu'au tombeau soumise à sa tutelle
110 Jamais les feux d'hymen ne s'allument pour elle.
Dois-je épouser ses droits contre un père irrité ?
Donnerai-je l'exemple à la témérité ?
Et dans un fol amour ma jeunesse embarquée . . .

THÉRAMÈNE

Ah, Seigneur ! Si votre heure est une fois marquée,
Le Ciel de nos raisons ne sait point s'informer.
Thésée ouvre vos yeux en voulant les fermer,
Et sa haine irritant une flamme rebelle,
Prête à son ennemie une grâce nouvelle.
Enfin d'un chaste amour pourquoi vous effrayer ?
120 S'il a quelque douceur n'osez-vous l'essayer ?
En croirez-vous toujours un farouche scrupule ?
Craint-on de s'égarer sur les traces d'Hercule ?
Quels courages Vénus n'a-t-elle pas domptés !
Vous-même où seriez-vous, vous qui la combattez,
Si toujours Antiope à ses lois opposée
D'une pudique ardeur n'eût brûlé pour Thésée ?
Mais que sert d'affecter un superbe discours ?
Avouez-le, tout change. Et depuis quelques jours
On vous voit moins souvent, orgueilleux, et sauvage
130 Tantôt faire voler un char sur le rivage,
Tantôt savant dans l'art par Neptune inventé,
Rendre docile au frein un coursier indompté.
Les forêts de nos cris moins souvent retentissent.
Chargés d'un feu secret vos yeux s'appesantissent.

Degraded to the same indignity?
—Baseness beyond excuse, for those were frailties
100 Unseen amid a multitude of honours,
While not one trophy of a monster slain
Entitles me to fail as he has failed.
Even if I lost my freedom and my pride
How could I yield them to Aricia?
How could my disobedient sense forget
That which divides us irremovably?
The King denies her, denies her fallen brothers,
By violent laws, continuance of their line;
Their name must die for ever in her death,
110 Their guilty branch must bear no other fruit,
And till the tomb, submissive and sequestered,
No gleam of the Hymeneal torch must find her.
Am I to oppose my father and his wrath?
Embrace her claims? and give a precedent
To treason? and embark my youth—

THERAMENES

My lord,
If the marked hour draws on, our arguments
Escape the notice of the incurious Heavens.
No. Theseus wished you blind, and gave you eyes;
His hate inflames the passion he forbids you,
120 And adds enchantment to his prisoner's charms.
But come, why look askance at honest love?
Why not make trial where its sweetness lies?
Why be enchained by vain and foolish scruples?
Who fears to stray that follows Hercules?
Many a stubborn heart has Venus bent—
Where would you be yourself and your defiance
Had chaste Antiope been as chaste as you
And never warmed to Theseus' flame? But why
Face out a falsehood with the pride of words?
130 Confess how things have changed: not now as once,
Aloof, intractable, we see you guide
A skimming chariot along the beaches
Or, adept in the mystery Neptune taught,
Break an unmastered courser to the curb;
Less often our halloos awake the forests;
Your eyes droop, weighted with a secret fire . . .

Il n'en faut point douter, vous aimez, vous brûlez.
Vous périssez d'un mal que vous dissimulez.
La charmante Aricie a-t-elle su vous plaire ?

HIPPOLYTE

Théramène, je pars, et vais chercher mon père.

THÉRAMÈNE

Ne verrez-vous point Phèdre avant que de partir,
140 Seigneur ?

HIPPOLYTE

                    C'est mon dessein, tu peux l'en avertir.
Voyons-la, puisqu'ainsi mon devoir me l'ordonne.
Mais quel nouveau malheur trouble sa chère Œnone ?

SCÈNE II

HIPPOLYTE, ŒNONE, THÉRAMÈNE

ŒNONE

Hélas, Seigneur ! quel trouble au mien peut être égal ?
La Reine touche presque à son terme fatal.
En vain à l'observer jour et nuit je m'attache.
Elle meurt dans mes bras d'un mal qu'elle me cache.
Un désordre éternel règne dans son esprit.
Son chagrin inquiet l'arrache de son lit.
Elle veut voir le jour ; Et sa douleur profonde
150 M'ordonne toutefois d'écarter tout le monde . . .
Elle vient.

HIPPOLYTE

                    Il suffit, je la laisse en ces lieux,
Et ne lui montre point un visage odieux.

SCÈNE III

PHÈDRE, ŒNONE

PHÈDRE

N'allons point plus avant. Demeurons, chère Œnone.
Je ne me soutiens plus, ma force m'abandonne.
Mes yeux sont éblouis du jour que je revoi,
Et mes genoux tremblants se dérobent sous moi.
Hélas !   *Elle s'assit.*

ŒNONE

                    Dieux tout-puissants ! que nos pleurs vous apaisent.

The case is clear—you are in love, in flame,
In torment, and you will not show your wound.
Is it Aricia?

HIPPOLYTUS

Theramenes,

140 I leave to-day, and go to find my father.

THERAMENES

Without an audience of Phaedra?

HIPPOLYTUS

No.

I will see her; I cannot well do less.
You may send word.—But what is the fresh misfortune
Disturbs her favourite Oenone so?

Enter OENONE

OENONE

Ah, good my lord, what grief can equal mine?
The Queen is near her utmost bourne of fate;
She that I watch by night and day unsleeping
Dies in my arms, and will not tell her sickness.
Her thought is all at variance with itself;

150 Her sick disquiet drives her from her bed
To see the light of day. But by her orders
No eye of man may see her suffering.
—Here she is.

HIPPOLYTUS

Very well; then I retire
Not to offend with this unwelcome face.

Exeunt HIPPOLYTUS & THERAMENES

Enter PHAEDRA

PHAEDRA

No more, for I can move no more, Oenone.
Let me rest; I am faint, my strength has left me.
My darkened eyes are dazzled by the light,
My wavering knees are weak beneath my weight.
Ah me!   *Sits*

OENONE

High Gods, relent and see our tears!

PHÈDRE

Que ces vains ornements, que ces voiles me pèsent !
Quelle importune main, en formant tous ces nœuds,
160 A pris soin sur mon front d'assembler mes cheveux ?
Tout m'afflige et me nuit, et conspire à me nuire.

ŒNONE

Comme on voit tous ses vœux l'un l'autre se détruire !
Vous-même condamnant vos injustes desseins,
Tantôt à vous parer vous excitiez nos mains.
Vous-même rappelant votre force première
Vous vouliez vous montrer et revoir la lumière ;
Vous la voyez, Madame, et prête à vous cacher,
Vous haïssez le jour que vous veniez chercher ?

PHÈDRE

Noble et brillant auteur d'une triste famille,
170 Toi, dont ma mère osait se vanter d'être fille,
Qui peut-être rougis du trouble où tu me vois,
Soleil, je te viens voir pour la dernière fois.

ŒNONE

Quoi ! vous ne perdrez point cette cruelle envie ?
Vous verrai-je toujours renonçant à la vie
Faire de votre mort les funestes apprêts ?

PHÈDRE

Dieux ! Que ne suis-je assise à l'ombre des forêts !
Quand pourrai-je au travers d'une noble poussière
Suivre de l'œil un char fuyant dans la carrière ?

ŒNONE

Quoi, Madame !

PHÈDRE

      Insensée, où suis-je ? et qu'ai-je dit ?
180 Où laissé-je égarer mes vœux, et mon esprit ?
Je l'ai perdu. Les Dieux m'en ont ravi l'usage.
Œnone, la rougeur me couvre le visage,
Je te laisse trop voir mes honteuses douleurs,
Et mes yeux malgré moi se remplissent de pleurs.

ŒNONE

Ah ! s'il vous faut rougir, rougissez d'un silence,
Qui de vos maux encore aigrit la violence.
Rebelle à tous nos soins, sourde à tous nos discours,
Voulez-vous sans pitié laisser finir vos jours ?

PHAEDRA

160 These fripperies, these veils, they hang so heavy!
Whose was the unkind hand that piled and bound
These clustering locks that weigh upon my brow?
So feeble and so weary, all these things
Grieve me and weary me.

OENONE

How can we please you?
Yourself, repentant of your wicked thoughts,
You called in haste for clothes and ornaments;
Yourself you rallied your forgotten vigour,
You wanted to be out and see the sunlight.
Now here it is, my lady, and it seems
170 You loathe the very light that you desired.

PHAEDRA

Splendid begetter of a seed afflicted,
Father from whom my mother claimed her birth,
O blushing Sun ashamed of my despair,
Now, for the last time, I salute thy face.

OENONE

What, still possessed of such a fearful purpose?
Shall I for ever see you, turned from life,
Enact the mournful ritual of your death?

PHAEDRA

Oh give me the shadow of the forest glades!
Or let my eye piercing the glorious dust
180 Follow the wheeling chariot in the course!

OENONE

My lady?

PHAEDRA

Oh, I am mad. What have I said?
Where am I, where are my thoughts, my wandering mind?
Lost, for the Gods have taken it away.
My face is hot, Oenone, with my shame;
I cannot hide my guilty sufferings
And tears descend that I cannot restrain.

OENONE

Blush if you must, but blush to keep a silence
That doubles all the misery you suffer.
Rebellious to all tending, deaf to all pleas,
190 Will you unpitying allow your life

Quelle fureur les borne au milieu de leur course ?
190 Quel charme ou quel poison en a tari la source ?
Les ombres par trois fois ont obscurci les cieux,
Depuis que le sommeil n'est entré dans vos yeux;
Et le jour a trois fois chassé la nuit obscure,
Depuis que votre corps languit sans nourriture.
A quel affreux dessein vous laissez-vous tenter ?
De quel droit sur vous-même osez-vous attenter ?
Vous offensez les Dieux auteurs de votre vie.
Vous trahissez l'époux à qui la foi vous lie,
Vous trahissez enfin vos enfants malheureux,
200 Que vous précipitez sous un joug rigoureux.
Songez qu'un même jour leur ravira leur mère,
Et rendra l'espérance au fils de l'étrangère,
A ce fier ennemi de vous, de votre sang,
Ce fils qu'une Amazone a porté dans son flanc,
Cet Hippolyte . . .

> PHÈDRE

Ah Dieux !

> ŒNONE

Ce reproche vous touche.

> PHÈDRE

Malheureuse, quel nom est sorti de ta bouche ?

> ŒNONE

Hé bien, votre colère éclate avec raison.
J'aime à vous voir frémir à ce funeste nom.
Vivez donc. Que l'amour, le devoir vous excite.
210 Vivez, ne souffrez pas que le fils d'une Scythe,
Accablant vos enfants d'un empire odieux,
Commande au plus beau sang de la Grèce, et des Dieux.
Mais ne différez point, chaque moment vous tue.
Réparez promptement votre force abattue,
Tandis que de vos jours prêts à se consumer
Le flambeau dure encore, et peut se rallumer.

> PHÈDRE

J'en ai trop prolongé la coupable durée.

> ŒNONE

Quoi ! de quelques remords êtes-vous déchirée ?
Quel crime a pu produire un trouble si pressant ?
220 Vos mains n'ont point trempé dans le sang innocent ?

To flow away? What madness cuts it short?
What spell, what poison stanches up its course?
Thrice has the sky been muffled up in shade
And sleep is still a stranger to your eyes;
Thrice has the day displaced the gloom of night
And still you fast, and still your body wastes.
What dark temptation leads you on? What right
Invests you with the power to take your life—
Wronging the Gods from whom you draw your being,
200 Failing the husband who received your promise,
Failing still more your helpless children, doomed
To bitter lives of bondage: for reflect,
The very day that takes their mother from them
Rebuilds the hope of that Barbarian's child,
That arrogant enemy of you and yours,
The boy the Amazonian stranger bore
Hippolytus—

PHAEDRA

O Gods!

OENONE

That charge strikes home!

PHAEDRA

Woman, how dare you name that name to me?

OENONE

Why, now your anger is most justly roused.
210 It heartens me that you should shrink to hear
That fatal name. Then live. For love, for duty,
Live; if you would not have the Scythian's son,
Bending your children to his hated yoke,
Lord it over the fairest blood of Greece
And of the Gods. But do not wait, each moment
You die. Rally, betimes, your prostrate vigour
While yet your almost spent and guttering life
Still glows, and may be kindled once again.

PHAEDRA

I have outlived the right to live already.

OENONE

220 Why, is there some remorse that feeds upon you?
What have you done that drives you so distraught?
your hands have never dipped in guiltless blood?

PHÈDRE

Grâces au Ciel, mes mains ne sont point criminelles.
Plût aux Dieux que mon cœur fût innocent comme elles !

ŒNONE

Et quel affreux projet avez-vous enfanté,
Dont votre cœur encor doive être épouvanté ?

PHÈDRE

Je t'en ai dit assez. Épargne-moi le reste.
Je meurs, pour ne point faire un aveu si funeste.

ŒNONE

Mourez donc, et gardez un silence inhumain.
Mais pour fermer vos yeux cherchez une autre main.
Quoiqu'il vous reste à peine une faible lumière,
230 Mon âme chez les morts descendra la première.
Mille chemins ouverts y conduisent toujours,
Et ma juste douleur choisira les plus courts.
Cruelle, quand ma foi vous a-t-elle déçue ?
Songez-vous qu'en naissant mes bras vous ont reçue ?
Mon pays, mes enfants, pour vous j'ai tout quitté.
Réserviez-vous ce prix à ma fidélité ?

PHÈDRE

Quel fruit espères-tu de tant de violence ?
Tu frémiras d'horreur si je romps le silence.

ŒNONE

Et que me direz-vous, qui ne cède, grands Dieux !
240 A l'horreur de vous voir expirer à mes yeux ?

PHÈDRE

Quand tu sauras mon crime, et le sort qui m'accable,
Je n'en mourrai pas moins, j'en mourrai plus coupable.

ŒNONE

Madame, au nom des pleurs que pour vous j'ai versés,
Par vos faibles genoux que je tiens embrassés,
Délivrez mon esprit de ce funeste doute.

PHÈDRE

Tu le veux. Lève-toi.

ŒNONE

                    Parlez. Je vous écoute.

PHÈDRE

Ciel ! que lui vais-je dire ? Et par où commencer ?

PHAEDRA

I thank the Gods my hands are free of evil.
Would that my heart were innocent as they!

OENONE

What resolution, then, have you conceived
To terrify your heart before the time?

PHAEDRA

I have said enough. Ask me no more, have pity;
For if I die it is to keep within me
This dreadful secret.

OENONE

                  Keep it then, and die;

230 But other hands, not mine, will close your eyes.
Yours is a weak and flickering fire, but I
Will lose my spirit first among the dead;
There are many avenues and all unbarred;
An injured heart will soon perceive the best.—
Ungrateful mistress, when did I betray you?
Have you forgotten that these hands received you
When you were born? My children and my home,
I have left all for you: and all for this.

PHAEDRA

What do you think to gain by this beseeching?

240 You will shrink with horror if I break my silence.

OENONE

What can you tell me then more horrible
Than thus to see you die before my face?

PHAEDRA

And when you know my destiny and my weakness
Still I shall die, and only die more guilty.

OENONE

My lady, by the tears I shed for you,
By these your trembling knees I hold entwined,
Deliver me from deadly fear and doubt.

PHAEDRA

You wish it. Rise.

OENONE

             Speak on, and I will listen.

PHAEDRA

How shall I tell, ye Gods, or where begin?

ŒNONE

Par de vaines frayeurs cessez de m'offenser.

PHÈDRE

O haine de Vénus! O fatale colère!
250 Dans quels égarements l'amour jeta ma mère!

ŒNONE

Oublions-les, Madame. Et qu'à tout l'avenir
Un silence éternel cache ce souvenir.

PHÈDRE

Ariane, ma sœur! De quel amour blessée,
Vous mourûtes aux bords où vous fûtes laissée!

ŒNONE

Que faites-vous, Madame? Et quel mortel ennui,
Contre tout votre sang vous anime aujourd'hui?

PHÈDRE

Puisque Vénus le veut, de ce sang déplorable
Je péris la dernière, et la plus misérable.

ŒNONE

Aimez-vous?

PHÈDRE

           De l'amour j'ai toutes les fureurs.

ŒNONE

260 Pour qui?

PHÈDRE

         Tu vas ouïr le comble des horreurs.
J'aime . . . à ce nom fatal, je tremble, je frissonne.
J'aime . . .

ŒNONE

        Qui?

PHÈDRE

          Tu connais ce fils de l'Amazone,
Ce Prince si longtemps par moi-même opprimé.

ŒNONE

Hippolyte! Grands Dieux!

PHÈDRE

                C'est toi qui l'as nommé.

ŒNONE

Juste ciel! tout mon sang dans mes veines se glace.
O désespoir! O crime! O déplorable race!
Voyage infortuné! Rivage malheureux!
Fallait-il approcher de tes bords dangereux?

OENONE

250 Your fears are insults to my loyalty.

PHAEDRA

O deathless hate of Venus, fatal vengeance!
O heavy doom of love upon my mother!

OENONE

Forget, my lady. Hide that memory
And keep it from the ears of later times.

PHAEDRA

Love left thee dying, sweet sister Ariadne,
Lying forsaken by the alien waters.

OENONE

Let be, my lady. Must your mortal grief
Be vented on the dearest of your blood?

PHAEDRA

Of this doomed blood, I, by the will of Venus,

260 I perish now the last and most accursed.

OENONE

You love!

PHAEDRA

    To madness and to ecstasy.

OENONE

Whom?

PHAEDRA

   There's the horror that surpasses horror:
I love . . . at the fatal name I blench and tremble—
I love . . .

OENONE

    But whom?

PHAEDRA

       You know the Amazon's son,
The young Prince who endured so much, through me . . .

OENONE

O Gods! Hippolytus!

PHAEDRA

      You spoke the name!

OENONE

Sweet Heavens! You have chilled my very blood.
O race polluted, hopeless, lamentable!
Woe worth the day that brought us to these shores!

270 Why did we venture?

PHÈDRE

Mon mal vient de plus loin. A peine au fils d'Égée,
270 Sous les lois de l'hymen je m'étais engagée,
Mon repos, mon bonheur semblait être affermi,
Athènes me montra mon superbe ennemi.
Je le vis, je rougis, je pâlis à sa vue.
Un trouble s'éleva dans mon âme éperdue.
Mes yeux ne voyaient plus, je ne pouvais parler,
Je sentis tout mon corps et transir, et brûler.
Je reconnus Vénus, et ses feux redoutables,
D'un sang qu'elle poursuit tourments inévitables.
Par des vœux assidus je crus les détourner,
280 Je lui bâtis un temple, et pris soin de l'orner.
De victimes moi-même à toute heure entourée,
Je cherchais dans leurs flancs ma raison égarée,
D'un incurable amour remèdes impuissants !
En vain sur les autels ma main brûlait l'encens.
Quand ma bouche implorait le nom de la Déesse,
J'adorais Hippolyte, et le voyant sans cesse,
Même au pied des autels que je faisais fumer,
J'offrais tout à ce Dieu, que je n'osais nommer.
Je l'évitais partout. O comble de misère !
290 Mes yeux le retrouvaient dans les traits de son père.
Contre moi-même enfin j'osai me révolter.
J'excitai mon courage à le persécuter.
Pour bannir l'ennemi dont j'étais idolâtre,
J'affectai les chagrins d'une injuste marâtre,
Je pressai son exil, et mes cris éternels
L'arrachèrent du sein, et des bras paternels.
Je respirais, Œnone; et depuis son absence
Mes jours moins agités coulaient dans l'innocence.
Soumise à mon époux, et cachant mes ennuis,
300 De son fatal hymen je cultivais les fruits.
Vaines précautions ! Cruelle destinée !
Par mon époux lui-même à Trézène amenée
J'ai revu l'ennemi que j'avais éloigné.
Ma blessure trop vive aussitôt a saigné.
Ce n'est plus une ardeur dans mes veines cachée;
C'est Vénus toute entière à sa proie attachée.
J'ai conçu pour mon crime une juste terreur.
J'ai pris la vie en haine, et ma flamme en horreur.

PHAEDRA

It was long ago
And far from here. When first the rite of Hymen
Bound my obedience to the son of Aegeus—
My happiness, my peace then seemed so plain—
Careless in Athens stood my conqueror.
I saw and gazed, I blushed and paled again,
A blind amazement rose and blurred my mind;
My eyes were dim, my lips forgot to speak,
This, I knew, was the awful flame of Venus,
The fated torment of her chosen victims.
280 I tried to ward it off with prayers, with vows
And offerings, a temple built and decked,
And in the midst of endless sacrifices
I searched the entrails for my erring wisdom.
Weak drugs for irremediable love!
Even as my hand spilt incense at the shrine,
Even as my lips invoked the name of Venus
I prayed Hippolytus, my eyes beheld
Hippolytus, and while the altars steamed
I offered all to him I dared not name.
290 I fled him everywhere. O bitterness,
He looked upon me in his father's features.
At last, I turned upon myself. I forced
Myself to play the torturer against
The dreaded enemy I loved too well,
Put on the bride's abhorrence of the stepson,
Pleaded and pressed until I banished him
Out of his father's arms, his father's heart.
Once more I breathed; and after this, Oenone,
My life, serener, flowed in blameless ways,
300 Pleasing my husband, covering my pain,
Tending the fruits of his unhappy bed:
Foolish expedients! and inexorable
Hardness of destiny!—My lord himself
Brought me to Trozen and my banished foe.
The ancient wound gaped deep, and bled again.
No longer is it a secret flame that flickers
About my veins: headlong in onset Venus
Hangs on her quarry! I abhorred my guilt,
Life was a curse, my love a misery;

Je voulais en mourant prendre soin de ma gloire,
310 Et dérober au jour une flamme si noire.
Je n'ai pu soutenir tes larmes, tes combats.
Je t'ai tout avoué, je ne m'en repens pas,
Pourvu que de ma mort respectant les approches
Tu ne m'affliges plus par d'injustes reproches,
Et que tes vains secours cessent de rappeler
Un reste de chaleur, tout prêt à s'exhaler.

SCÈNE IV
PHÈDRE, ŒNONE, PANOPE

PANOPE

Je voudrais vous cacher une triste nouvelle,
Madame. Mais il faut que je vous la révèle.
La mort vous a ravi votre invincible époux,
320 Et ce malheur n'est plus ignoré que de vous.

ŒNONE
Panope, que dis-tu ?

PANOPE
                    Que la Reine abusée
En vain demande au Ciel le retour de Thésée,
Et que par des vaisseaux arrivés dans le port
Hippolyte son fils vient d'apprendre sa mort.

PHÈDRE
Ciel !

PANOPE
        Pour le choix d'un maître Athènes se partage.
Au Prince votre fils l'un donne son suffrage,
Madame, et de l'État l'autre oubliant les lois
Au fils de l'étrangère ose donner sa voix.
On dit même qu'au trône une brigue insolente
330 Veut placer Aricie, et le sang de Pallante.
J'ai cru de ce péril vous devoir avertir.
Déjà même Hippolyte est tout prêt à partir,
Et l'on craint, s'il paraît dans ce nouvel orage,
Qu'il ne'ntraîne après lui tout un peuple volage.

ŒNONE
Panope, c'est assez. La Reine qui t'entend,
Ne négligera point cet avis important.

310 I looked for death to save my name, and bury
Far from the day the darkness of these fires.
I could not face your strivings and your tears.
Now you know all; and it is well, if you
Stand but aside from my advancing death,
Abstain at last from undeserved reproaches,
And leave your useless effort to revive
The embers of a fast-expiring fire.

Enter PANOPE

PANOPE
I wish that I could hide the news, my lady,
That I am forced to bring you. Death has taken
320 Your lord, our most indomitable King;
And you alone are ignorant of your loss.
OENONE
What is this, Panope?
PANOPE
            My lady's prayers
Will never now bring Theseus back to Athens,
And mariners that landed here to-day
Have told Hippolytus that he is dead.
PHAEDRA
Gods!
PANOPE
            Athens wavers in the choice of masters.
One boasts allegiance to the Prince your son;
One, reckless of the statutes of the land,
Presumes to favour the Barbarian's child,
330 My lady; and they say a rank sedition
Proclaims Aricia and the blood of Pallas.
I knew it was my duty to report
Such perils. Even now Hippolytus
Embarks, and many fear if he arrives
In this tempestuous season, he will sway
A shifting multitude.
OENONE
            Panope, thank you:
Your news was precious, and the Queen has heard.
Exit PANOPE

SCÈNE V

PHÈDRE, ŒNONE

ŒNONE

Madame, je cessais de vous presser de vivre.
Déjà même au tombeau je songeais à vous suivre.
Pour vous en détourner je n'avais plus de voix.
340 Mais ce nouveau malheur vous prescrit d'autres lois.
Votre fortune change et prend une autre face.
Le Roi n'est plus, Madame, il faut prendre sa place.
Sa mort vous laisse un fils à qui vous vous devez,
Esclave, s'il vous perd, et Roi, si vous vivez.
Sur qui dans son malheur voulez-vous qu'il s'appuie ?
Ses larmes n'auront plus de main qui les essuie.
Et ses cris innocents portés jusques aux Dieux,
Iront contre sa mère irriter ses aïeux.
Vivez, vous n'avez plus de reproche à vous faire.
350 Votre flamme devient une flamme ordinaire.
Thésée en expirant vient de rompre les nœuds,
Qui faisaient tout le crime et l'horreur de vos feux.
Hippolyte pour vous devient moins redoutable,
Et vous pouvez le voir sans vous rendre coupable.
Peut-être convaincu de votre aversion
Il va donner un chef à la sédition.
Détrompez son erreur, fléchissez son courage.
Roi de ces bords heureux, Trézène est son partage.
Mais il sait que les lois donnent à votre fils
360 Les superbes remparts que Minerve a bâtis.
Vous avez l'un et l'autre une juste ennemie.
Unissez-vous tous deux pour combattre Aricie.

PHÈDRE

Hé bien ! A tes conseils je me laisse entraîner,
Vivons, si vers la vie on peut me ramener,
Et si l'amour d'un fils en ce moment funeste
De mes faibles esprits peut ranimer le reste.

Fin du premier Acte

OENONE

My lady, I had thrown away all pleadings,
All hope to move you, and my only thought
340 Was to attend you past the gates of the tomb.
But new disaster points new purposes,
An altered fortune, and an altered duty.

Theseus is dead, and you are his successor,
My lady, with a son that looks to you—
A slave alone, and if you live, a King.
No other will uphold his friendless quarrel,
No other wipe away his orphan tears;
Only in Heaven will his hearers be
The Gods, your judges and his ancestors.
350 Live then, in liberty from all misgiving;
Your love is now as unremarkable
As any love, for death disjoins the bond
That made its foulness and its infamy.
Henceforth the image of Hippolytus
Is not so terrible, and you may see him
With perfect guiltlessness. But what if now,
Despairing of a better understanding,
He takes command of these rebellious throngs?
Open his eyes, soften that stubborn heart.
360 Prince of these smiling coasts, his patrimony
Is here in Trozen, but he knows the laws;
He knows that they deliver to your son
The queenly ramparts that Minerva reared.
Your rightful enemy is also his:
Unite your forces to defeat Aricia.

PHAEDRA

So be it. I commit my way to you.
I will live, if I still have strength to live
And if a mother's love can even now
Revive in my wasted flesh the seeds of life.

Acte II

SCÈNE PREMIÈRE
ARICIE, ISMÈNE

ARICIE
Hippolyte demande à me voir en ce lieu ?
Hippolyte me cherche, et veut me dire adieu ?
Ismène, dis-tu vrai ? N'es-tu point abusée ?
ISMÈNE
370 C'est le premier effet de la mort de Thésée.
Préparez-vous, Madame, à voir de tous côtés
Voler vers vous les cœurs par Thésée écartés.
Aricie à la fin de son sort est maîtresse,
Et bientôt à ses pieds verra toute la Grèce.
ARICIE
Ce n'est donc point, Ismène, un bruit mal affermi ?
Je cesse d'être esclave, et n'ai plus d'ennemi ?
ISMÈNE
Non, Madame, les Dieux ne vous sont plus contraires,
Et Thésée a rejoint les mânes de vos frères.
ARICIE
Dit-on quelle aventure a terminé ses jours ?
ISMÈNE
380 On sème de sa mort d'incroyables discours.
On dit que ravisseur d'une amante nouvelle
Les flots ont englouti cet époux infidèle.
On dit même, et ce bruit est partout répandu,
Qu'avec Pirithoüs aux Enfers descendu
Il a vu le Cocyte et les rivages sombres,
Et s'est montré vivant aux infernales ombres ;
Mais qu'il n'a pu sortir de ce triste séjour,
Et repasser les bords, qu'on passe sans retour.

Act Two

ARICIA, ISMENE

ARICIA

370 He asked to see me here? Hippolytus
     Wanted to see me and to say farewell?
     Are you quite certain? Is this true, Ismene?

ISMENE

     Much more than this, now that the King is dead.
     Prepare yourself, my lady; all the hearts
     He kept at bay will cluster at your feet.
     All Greece will bring its tribute to Aricia,
     Enfranchised now and sovereign of her fortunes.

ARICIA

     So then, Ismene, it is no idle talk
     And I have no oppressor and no foe?

ISMENE

380 My lady, none. The Heavens have relented
     And Theseus walks among your fathers' shades.

ARICIA

     What enterprise has brought him to his death?
     Do they say?

ISMENE

                 Rumours wild and past belief:
     Some say that in a lover's last adventure
     The seas have claimed this ever-wandering husband;
     Some say, and everywhere the news is sown,
     That with Pirithous he went down to Hell,
     Saw the Cocytus and the coasts of darkness
     And stood alive amid a world of shadows,
390 But could not scale the gloomy track again
     Nor pass the bourne men never pass but once.

ARICIE

Croirai-je qu'un mortel avant sa dernière heure
390 Peut pénétrer des morts la profonde demeure ?
Quel charme l'attirait sur ces bords redoutés ?

ISMÈNE

Thésée est mort, Madame, et vous seule en doutez.
Athènes en gémit, Trézène en est instruite,
Et déjà pour son Roi reconnaît Hippolyte.
Phèdre dans ce palais tremblante pour son fils,
De ses amis troublés demande les avis.

ARICIE

Et tu crois que pour moi plus humain que son père
Hippolyte rendra ma chaîne plus légère ?
Qu'il plaindra mes malheurs ?

ISMÈNE

                              Madame, je le croi.

ARICIE

400 L'insensible Hippolyte est-il connu de toi ?
Sur quel frivole espoir penses-tu qu'il me plaigne,
Et respecte en moi seule un sexe qu'il dédaigne ?
Tu vois depuis quel temps il évite nos pas,
Et cherche tous les lieux où nous ne sommes pas.

ISMÈNE

Je sais de ses froideurs tout ce que l'on récite.
Mais j'ai vu près de vous ce superbe Hippolyte.
Et même, en le voyant, le bruit de sa fierté
A redoublé pour lui ma curiosité.
Sa présence à ce bruit n'a point paru répondre.
410 Dès vos premiers regards je l'ai vu se confondre.
Ses yeux, qui vainement voulaient vous éviter,
Déjà pleins de langueur ne pouvaient vous quitter.
Le nom d'amant peut-être offense son courage.
Mais il en a les yeux, s'il n'en a le langage.

ARICIE

Que mon cœur, chère Ismène, écoute avidement
Un discours, qui peut-être a peu de fondement !
O toi ! qui me connais, te semblait-il croyable
Que le triste jouet d'un sort impitoyable,
Un cœur toujours nourri d'amertume et de pleurs,
420 Dût connaître l'amour, et ses folles douleurs ?
Reste du sang d'un Roi, noble fils de la Terre,

ARICIA

Shall mortal men, before the last leave-taking,
Fathom those sullen deeps of the Departed?
What sorcery lured him to their awful shore?

ISMENE

My lady, he is dead, and you alone
Doubt it. All Athens grieves for him, all Trozen
Knows, and salutes Hippolytus for Prince.
And in these walls, despairing for her son,
Phaedra takes counsel of her trembling friends.

ARICIA

400 And you suppose that, kinder than his father,
Hippolytus will make my bondage sweeter
And pity me?

ISMENE

My lady, yes, I do.

ARICIA

But do you know the hard Hippolytus?
What makes you fancy he could feel compassion
For me alone, who never felt for woman?
He never joins our customary paths
And hides himself wherever we are not.

ISMENE

Oh, I know all the legend of his coldness;
But when you met the proud Hippolytus
410 I own the strangeness of his reputation
Sharpened the edge of my curiosity.
I saw a face at variance with the fable;
At once your eyes disturbed that hard assurance
And his, avoiding you but all in vain,
Melted at once, and could not turn away.
His pride may yet refuse the name of lover
But I'll believe his looks, and not his tongue.

ARICIA

Ah, sweet Ismene, how my heart devours
The unhoped-for comfort of a mere perhaps!
420 You that have known me, did you once imagine
This heart, the plaything of unpitying Fate,
Starved of all sustenance except despair,
Would learn of love and the wild woes of love?
Child of Earth's child, last of a royal lineage,

Je suis seule échappée aux fureurs de la guerre,
J'ai perdu dans la fleur de leur jeune saison
Six frères, quel espoir d'une illustre maison !
Le fer moissonna tout, et la Terre humectée
But à regret le sang des neveux d'Érechthée.
Tu sais depuis leur mort quelle sévère loi
Défend à tous les Grecs de soupirer pour moi.
On craint que de la sœur les flammes téméraires
430 Ne raniment un jour la cendre de ses frères.
Mais tu sais bien aussi de quel œil dédaigneux
Je regardais ce soin d'un vainqueur soupçonneux.
Tu sais que de tout temps à l'Amour opposée
Je rendais souvent grâce à l'injuste Thésée
Dont l'heureuse rigueur secondait mes mépris.
Mes yeux alors, mes yeux n'avaient pas vu son fils.
Non que par les yeux seuls lâchement enchantée
J'aime en lui sa beauté, sa grâce tant vantée,
Présents dont la Nature a voulu l'honorer,
440 Qu'il méprise lui-même, et qu'il semble ignorer.
J'aime, je prise en lui de plus nobles richesses,
Les vertus de son père, et non point les faiblesses.
J'aime, je l'avoûrai, cet orgueil généreux
Qui jamais n'a fléchi sous le joug amoureux.
Phèdre en vain s'honorait des soupirs de Thésée.
Pour moi, je suis plus fière, et fuis la gloire aisée
D'arracher un hommage à mille autres offert,
Et d'entrer dans un cœur de toutes parts ouvert.
Mais de faire fléchir un courage inflexible,
450 De porter la douleur dans une âme insensible,
D'enchaîner un captif de ses fers étonné,
Contre un joug qui lui plaît vainement mutiné ;
C'est là ce que je veux, c'est là ce qui m'irrite.
Hercule à désarmer coûtait moins qu'Hippolyte,
Et vaincu plus souvent, et plus tôt surmonté
Préparait moins de gloire aux yeux qui l'ont dompté.
Mais, chère Ismène, hélas ! quelle est mon imprudence !
On ne m'opposera que trop de résistance.
Tu m'entendras peut-être, humble dans mon ennui,
460 Gémir du même orgueil que j'admire aujourd'hui.
Hippolyte aimerait ? Par quel bonheur extrême
Aurais-je pu fléchir . . .

Sole remnant spared by battlefield and hatred,
I lost the last proud blossoms of our tree,
Six brothers, in the springtime of their year.
The steel reaped all, and Earth's unwilling furrows
Drank her own blood, the blood of her Erechtheus.
430 Since then you know what rigorous decree
Defies all Greeks to lift their eyes to mine—
For a mutinous ardour in the sister's breast
Might wake the embers in her brothers' urns—
And you remember how I laughed to scorn
Those calculations of the victor's fear;
I held that love itself was slavery
And even thanked the King for a constraint
So fit and favourable to my distaste—
Then, yes; but then I had not seen his son.
440 Not that subservient to the eye's seduction
I love him for that beauty, that demeanour,
Graces of partial Nature, gifts that he
Ignores, if ever he has noticed them;
I see richer and dearer treasures in him—
His father's parts, and not his father's failings;
For I confess I love the manly pride
That never bent under the yoke of love.
Phaedra was flattered by the doubtful glory
Of Theseus' courtly sighs: but I am prouder
450 And will not stoop to share an easy prize
Or occupy an undefended heart.
No, but to shape a will as yet unbending,
To waken pain in a proof-armoured bosom,
To lead a slave that never thought to serve,
Vainly at war against the pleasing chain—
There's a reward worthy of my ambition;
Hercules was an easier adversary
Who readily disarmed and quick to yield
Lent no such lustre to his overthrow.
460 But dear Ismene, these are reckless dreams:
Resistance there will be, and all too stubborn,
And you shall hear me soon in humbler strain
Lament the coldness that I praise to-day.
He love, Hippolytus? What height of fortune
Could ever bring him—

ISMÈNE

                              Vous l'entendrez lui-même.
Il vient à vous.

SCÈNE II
HIPPOLYTE, ARICIE, ISMÈNE

HIPPOLYTE

                    Madame, avant que de partir,
J'ai cru de votre sort vous devoir avertir.
Mon père ne vit plus. Ma juste défiance
Présageait les raisons de sa trop longue absence.
La mort seule bornant ses travaux éclatants
Pouvait à l'univers le cacher si longtemps.
Les Dieux livrent enfin à la Parque homicide
470 L'Ami, le Compagnon, le Successeur d'Alcide.
Je crois que votre haine, épargnant ses vertus,
Écoute sans regret ces noms qui lui sont dus.
Un espoir adoucit ma tristesse mortelle.
Je puis vous affranchir d'une austère tutelle.
Je révoque des lois dont j'ai plaint la rigueur,
Vous pouvez disposer de vous, de votre cœur.
Et dans cette Trézène aujourd'hui mon partage,
De mon aïeul Pitthée autrefois l'héritage,
Qui m'a sans balancer reconnu pour son Roi,
480 Je vous laisse aussi libre, et plus libre que moi.

ARICIE

Modérez des bontés, dont l'excès m'embarrasse.
D'un soin si généreux honorer ma disgrâce,
Seigneur, c'est me ranger, plus que vous ne pensez,
Sous ces austères lois, dont vous me dispensez.

HIPPOLYTE

Du choix d'un successeur Athènes incertaine
Parle de vous, me nomme, et le fils de la Reine.

ARICIE

De moi, Seigneur ?

HIPPOLYTE

                    Je sais, sans vouloir me flatter,
Qu'une superbe loi semble me rejeter.
La Grèce me reproche une mère étrangère.
490 Mais si pour concurrent je n'avais que mon frère,

ISMENE
                              Only let him speak;
He is coming now.

Enter HIPPOLYTUS

HIPPOLYTUS
                              My lady, before I go
I owe you some account of my intentions.
My father's dead: and well enough my fears
Foretold the causes of his late home-coming—
470 Death only, and the closure of his toils
Could hold him from the world so long. His Gods
At last abandon to the fatal Spinners
Alcides' friend, his fellow, his successor.
—I know your enmity will not forbid
His son to assert these titles he has earned.—
One hope alleviates my deepest sorrow,
For I can end a harsh and long subjection:
I here revoke laws that have caused me grief—
The full bestowal of your life and hand
480 Is yours alone, and in my patrimony,
This Trozen, seat of Pittheus my grandfather,
Which willingly defers his crown to me
I leave you free—, and freer than its Prince.
       ARICIA
Show me less kindness, I could bear it better.
So much regard for me in my abjection
Binds me, my lord, more even than you know,
To that constraint you would have put away.
       HIPPOLYTUS
Doubtful who stands the next in title, Athens
Canvasses you, and me, and Phaedra's son.
       ARICIA
490 Me, my lord?
       HIPPOLYTUS
                              I have never shut my eyes
To arrogant laws that seem to bar my claim:
The Greeks reject me for my mother's race.
But if my only rival were my brother
I can appeal to certain natural laws

Madame, j'ai sur lui de véritables droits
Que je saurais sauver du caprice des lois.
Un frein plus légitime arrête mon audace.
Je vous cède, ou plutôt je vous rends une place,
Un sceptre, que jadis vos aïeux ont reçu
De ce fameux mortel que la Terre a conçu.
L'adoption le mit entre les mains d'Égée.
Athènes par mon père accrue, et protégée
Reconnut avec joie un Roi si généreux,
500 Et laissa dans l'oubli vos frères malheureux.
Athènes dans ses murs maintenant vous rappelle.
Assez elle a gémi d'une longue querelle,
Assez dans ses sillons votre sang englouti
A fait fumer le champ dont il était sorti.
Trézène m'obéit. Les campagnes de Crète
Offrent au fils de Phèdre une riche retraite.
L'Attique est votre bien. Je pars, et vais pour vous
Réunir tous les vœux partagés entre nous.

ARICIE

De tout ce que j'entends étonnée et confuse
510 Je crains presque, je crains qu'un songe ne m'abuse.
Veillé-je? Puis-je croire un semblable dessein?
Quel Dieu, Seigneur, quel Dieu l'a mis dans votre sein?
Qu'à bon droit votre gloire en tous lieux est semée!
Et que la vérité passe la renommée!
Vous-même en ma faveur vous voulez vous trahir?
N'était-ce pas assez de ne me point haïr?
Et d'avoir si longtemps pu défendre votre âme
De cette inimitié . . .

HIPPOLYTE

                    Moi, vous haïr, Madame?
Avec quelques couleurs qu'on ait peint ma fierté,
520 Croit-on que dans ses flancs un Monstre m'ait porté?
Quelles sauvages mœurs, quelle haine endurcie
Pourrait, en vous voyant, n'être point adoucie?
Ai-je pu résister au charme décevant . . .

ARICIE

Quoi, Seigneur?

HIPPOLYTE

                    Je me suis engagé trop avant.
Je vois que la raison cède à la violence.

And make them good against the law's caprice.
I have a better reason to refrain—
To you I yield, say rather I restore,
The seat, the sceptre, that your fathers held
Of the illustrious mortal, son of Earth.
500 It only passed to Aegeus by adoption;
And next my father, Athens' second founder,
Was hailed and crowned for all his benefits
While your unhappy brothers lay forgot.
Now, Athens calls you home within her ramparts.
Too long the ancient quarrel lives in pain,
Too long your blood, shed on the Attic soil,
Reeks from the furrows where it found its birth.—
Trozen I hold. As for the son of Phaedra
The Cretan acres yield him rich retirement.
510 Attica falls to you. I sail, to join
Your partisans with mine, to serve your cause.

ARICIA

At every word more troubled and bewildered,
Can I, or dare I, think I heard you rightly?
Have I my senses, is this your intent?
What God, my lord, what God inspired your mind?
Rightly your glory sounds in every climate
But reputation falls behind the truth.
What, will you cheat yourself on my behalf?
It was enough indeed to think that you
520 Hated me not, and held a mind untainted
By this long enmity—

HIPPOLYTUS

              How could I hate you?
Men may deride this proud unconquered heart
But do they think a monster gave me birth?
What brutishness or what inveterate malice
Could see your face and not forget its fury?
And how should I withstand the subtle spell—

ARICIA

My lord! . . .

HIPPOLYTUS

       My tongue has carried me too far;
But wisdom fails and yields to the compulsion . . .

Puisque j'ai commencé de rompre le silence,
Madame, il faut poursuivre. Il faut vous informer
D'un secret, que mon cœur ne peut plus renfermer.
  Vous voyez devant vous un Prince déplorable,
530 D'un téméraire orgueil exemple mémorable.
Moi, qui contre l'Amour fièrement révolté,
Aux fers de ses captifs ai longtemps insulté,
Qui des faibles mortels déplorant les naufrages,
Pensais toujours du bord contempler les orages,
Asservi maintenant sous la commune loi,
Par quel trouble me vois-je emporté loin de moi !
Un moment a vaincu mon audace imprudente.
Cette âme si superbe est enfin dépendante.
Depuis près de six mois honteux, désespéré,
540 Portant partout le trait, dont je suis déchiré,
Contre vous, contre moi vainement je m'éprouve.
Présente je vous fuis, absente je vous trouve.
Dans le fond des forêts votre image me suit.
La lumière du jour, les ombres de la nuit,
Tout retrace à mes yeux les charmes que j'évite.
Tout vous livre à l'envi le rebelle Hippolyte.
Moi-même pour tout fruit de mes soins superflus,
Maintenant je me cherche, et ne me trouve plus.
Mon arc, mes javelots, mon char, tout m'importune.
550 Je ne me souviens plus des leçons de Neptune.
Mes seuls gémissements font retentir les bois,
Et mes coursiers oisifs ont oublié ma voix.
  Peut-être le récit d'un amour si sauvage
Vous fait en m'écoutant rougir de votre ouvrage.
D'un cœur qui s'offre à vous quel farouche entretien !
Quel étrange captif pour un si beau lien !
Mais l'offrande à vos yeux en doit être plus chère.
Songez que je vous parle une langue étrangère,
Et ne rejetez pas des vœux mal exprimés,
560 Qu'Hippolyte sans vous n'aurait jamais formés.

SCÈNE III
HIPPOLYTE, ARICIE, THÉRAMÈNE, ISMÈNE

THÉRAMÈNE
Seigneur, la Reine vient, et je l'ai devancée.
Elle vous cherche.

Now that my silence has been partly broken,
530 My lady, I must needs go on, and speak
The secret that my soul cannot contain.—
    Here stands a Prince of all men most unhappy,
A monument of overthrown presumption;
I, long a truant from the law of love
And long a mocker of its votaries,
That stayed ashore watching the luckless sailor
And never thought myself to fight the tempest,
Levelled at last beneath the common fate
By strange tides I am borne far from myself.
540 My wanton liberty has learnt to yield
And in an instant this bold heart was tamed.
Six months or nearly, in despair and shame,
I've borne the arrow burning in my side;
Vainly I pit my strength against myself
And you. I fly you where you are, and find you
Where you are not; deep in the forest glade
Your picture chases me; sunlight and dark
Alike retrace your features and alike
Betray the fugitive that would be free,
550 And I, for all my fruitless pains, look round
To find Hippolytus, and know him not.
My bow, my hounds, my spear, my chariot,
Weary me, Neptune's lessons are forgotten;
Only my lamentations fill the groves,
My stabled coursers know my voice no more.
    Perhaps this tale I tell of uncouth passion
Will make you blush to own your handiwork:
Wild terms, indeed, to offer up a heart!
And chains too fair for such a slave to claim!
560 And yet my tribute therefore ranks the higher;
Consider that I speak an unknown language
And do not spurn these faltered words of love
That you alone could teach Hippolytus.

Enter THERAMENES

THERAMENES
Close on my heels, my lord, the Queen approaches
Asking for you.

HIPPOLYTE

Moi !

THÉRAMÈNE

J'ignore sa pensée,
Mais on vous est venu demander de sa part.
Phèdre veut vous parler avant votre départ.

HIPPOLYTE

Phèdre ? Que lui dirai-je ? Et que peut-elle attendre . . .

ARICIE

Seigneur, vous ne pouvez refuser de l'entendre.
Quoique trop convaincu de son inimitié,
Vous devez à ses pleurs quelque ombre de pitié.

HIPPOLYTE

Cependant vous sortez. Et je pars. Et j'ignore
570 Si je n'offense point les charmes que j'adore.
J'ignore si ce cœur que je laisse en vos mains . . .

ARICIE

Partez, Prince, et suivez vos généreux desseins.
Rendez de mon pouvoir Athènes tributaire.
J'accepte tous les dons que vous me voulez faire.
Mais cet empire enfin si grand, si glorieux,
N'est pas de vos présents le plus cher à mes yeux.

SCÈNE IV
HIPPOLYTE, THÉRAMÈNE

HIPPOLYTE

Ami, tout est-il prêt ? Mais la Reine s'avance.
Va, que pour le départ tout s'arme en diligence.
Fais donner le signal, cours, ordonne, et revien
580 Me délivrer bientôt d'un fâcheux entretien.

SCÈNE V
PHÈDRE, HIPPOLYTE, ŒNONE

PHÈDRE *à Œnone*

Le voici. Vers mon cœur tout mon sang se retire.
J'oublie, en le voyant, ce que je viens lui dire.

ŒNONE

Souvenez-vous d'un fils qui n'espère qu'en vous.

HIPPOLYTUS
> For me?

THERAMENES
> > In what intention
I do not know, but messengers have come
Bidding you wait on her before you sail.

HIPPOLYTUS
The Queen? What should I say to her? Or she . . .

ARICIA
You cannot disappoint her wish, my lord.
570 Even to such an enemy is due
Some sign of formal pity for her grief.

HIPPOLYTUS
So you go. And I sail. And still I know not
Whether my worship has incensed my goddess,
Whether this heart I leave in your two hands . . .

ARICIA
Sail, Prince. Pursue your noble purposes;
Bring me the realm of Athens for dominion;
Whatever gift you make shall be accepted,
But that imperial and unhoped-for state
Is not the dearest of your offerings.
Exit ARICIA

HIPPOLYTUS
580 Good friend, are all things ready?—But I hear
The Queen.—Have all things ordered for our leaving.
Send out the signal. Haste, command, return
And free me from the burden of this meeting.
Exit THERAMENES.

Enter PHAEDRA and OENONE

PHAEDRA (*to Oenone*)
He is here. My blood retreats toward my heart.
I see him, and forget what I should speak.

OENONE
Be mindful of the son that trusts in you!

PHÈDRE

On dit qu'un prompt départ vous éloigne de nous,
Seigneur. A vos douleurs je viens joindre mes larmes.
Je vous viens pour un fils expliquer mes alarmes.
Mon fils n'a plus de père, et le jour n'est pas loin
Qui de ma mort encor doit le rendre témoin.
Déjà mille ennemis attaquent son enfance,
590 Vous seul pouvez contre eux embrasser sa défense.
Mais un secret remords agite mes esprits.
Je crains d'avoir fermé votre oreille à ses cris.
Je tremble que sur lui votre juste colère
Ne poursuive bientôt une odieuse mère.

HIPPOLYTE

Madame, je n'ai point des sentiments si bas.

PHÈDRE

Quand vous me haïriez je ne m'en plaindrais pas,
Seigneur. Vous m'avez vue attachée à vous nuire;
Dans le fond de mon cœur vous ne pouviez pas lire.
A votre inimitié j'ai pris soin de m'offrir.
600 Aux bords que j'habitais je n'ai pu vous souffrir.
En public, en secret contre vous déclarée,
J'ai voulu par des mers en être séparée.
J'ai même défendu par une expresse loi
Qu'on osât prononcer votre nom devant moi.
Si pourtant à l'offense on mesure la peine,
Si la haine peut seule attirer votre haine,
Jamais femme ne fut plus digne de pitié,
Et moins digne, Seigneur, de votre inimitié.

HIPPOLYTE

Des droits de ses enfants une mère jalouse
610 Pardonne rarement au fils d'une autre épouse.
Madame, je le sais. Les soupçons importuns
Sont d'un second hymen les fruits les plus communs.
Toute autre aurait pour moi pris les mêmes ombrages,
Et j'en aurais peut-être essuyé plus d'outrages.

PHAEDRA

They say that you are leaving us at once,
My lord. I came to join my grief with yours,
And with the story of a mother's terrors—
590 My child is fatherless, and soon the day
Will dawn that brings him to another deathbed;
So fiercely even now assailed and threatened,
Your strength alone can champion his weakness.—
But deep within me throbs the preying thought
That his complaint will never reach your ear,
That through my child your angry justice soon
Will strike a hated memory.

HIPPOLYTUS
                                              My lady,
So infamous a wish was never mine.

PHAEDRA

But you have seen me unremittingly
600 Pursue your hate, my lord; and how could you
Explore the bottom of my soul and read
My secret there? I threw myself upon
Your just resentment; I would not suffer you
Within the self-same frontiers; privily
And openly I waged my war, and set
The width of the sea between your path and mine.
I even gave explicit orders not
To breathe your name before my presence. Yet,
If by the wrong the penalty were measured,
610 If only hatred could achieve your hatred,
Never did woman more deserve your tears,
My lord, and less your enmity.

HIPPOLYTUS
                                        No mother
That watches for her children's interest
Forgives the other children of her house;
I know, my lady. Untoward mistrust
Is always near when men have married twice.
Another in your place would have conceived
No less suspicion, and I might have suffered
Deeper indignities.

PHÈDRE

Ah, Seigneur ! que le Ciel, j'ose ici l'attester,
De cette loi commune a voulu m'excepter !
Qu'un soin bien différent me trouble, et me dévore !

HIPPOLYTE

Madame, il n'est pas temps de vous troubler encore.
Peut-être votre époux voit encore le jour.
620 Le Ciel peut à nos pleurs accorder son retour.
Neptune le protège, et ce Dieu tutélaire
Ne sera pas en vain imploré par mon père.

PHÈDRE

On ne voit point deux fois le rivage des morts,
Seigneur. Puisque Thésée a vu les sombres bords,
En vain vous espérez qu'un Dieu vous le renvoie,
Et l'avare Achéron ne lâche point sa proie.
Que dis-je ? Il n'est point mort, puisqu'il respire en vous.
Toujours devant mes yeux je crois voir mon époux.
Je le vois, je lui parle, et mon cœur . . . Je m'égare,
630 Seigneur, ma folle ardeur malgré moi se déclare.

HIPPOLYTE

Je vois de votre amour l'effet prodigieux.
Tout mort qu'il est, Thésée est présent à vos yeux.
Toujours de son amour votre âme est embrasée.

PHÈDRE

Oui, Prince, le languis, je brûle pour Thésée.
Je l'aime, non point tel que l'ont vu les Enfers,
Volage adorateur de mille objets divers,
Qui va du Dieu des Morts déshonorer la couche;
Mais fidèle, mais fier, et même un peu farouche,
Charmant, jeune, traînant tous les cœurs après soi,
640 Tel qu'on dépeint nos Dieux, ou tel que je vous voi.
Il avait votre port, vos yeux, votre langage.
Cette noble pudeur colorait son visage,
Lorsque de notre Crète il traversa les flots,
Digne sujet des vœux des filles de Minos.
Que faisiez-vous alors : Pourquoi sans Hippolyte
Des héros de la Grèce assembla-t-il l'élite ?
Pourquoi trop jeune encor ne pûtes-vous alors
Entrer dans le vaisseau qui le mit sur nos bords ?

PHAEDRA

Ah but, my lord,

620 The Gods—as now they stand my witnesses—
Deigned to release me from this general law.
How different are the thoughts that ravage me!

HIPPOLYTUS

It is too soon, my lady, for such thoughts;
The sunshine may still light your husband's eye,
And Heaven still may yield him to our prayers;
For he will supplicate, and not in vain,
The love and the high patronage of Neptune.

PHAEDRA

No man has twice explored the coasts of Death,
My lord. If Theseus touched the sullen shores
630 Vainly we look for Gods to send him home:
Harsh Acheron is grasping and holds fast
His prey. But did I say that he is dead?
He breathes again in you; I see the King,
See him, speak to him, thrill . . . My mind is wandering,
My lord, my madness speaks the thing it should not.

HIPPOLYTUS

This is a prodigy of loyal love:
Theseus is gone, yet lives within your mind
And fires the ardour of your loving heart.

PHAEDRA

Yes, Prince, for him indeed I yearn, I languish;
640 I love him—not the man that Hell has claimed,
The butterfly that every beauty lured,
The adulterous ravisher that would have stained
The God of Hell's own bed; but faithful, fine,
Sometimes aloof, and pure, gallant and gay,
Young, stealing every heart upon his road—
So do they character our Gods, and so
I see you now; those eyes, that voice, were his,
That generous red of virtue in your cheek,
When first he drove across the Cretan foam,
650 Meet meditation for the virgin dreams
Of Minos' daughters. You, where were you then
Among the flower and chivalry of Greece?
Where was Hippolytus—alas, too young—
The day his vessel grounded on our shore?

Par vous aurait péri le Monstre de la Crète
650 Malgré tous les détours de sa vaste retraite.
Pour en développer l'embarras incertain
Ma sœur du fil fatal eût armé votre main.
Mais non, dans ce dessein je l'aurais devancée.
L'amour m'en eût d'abord inspiré la pensée.
C'est moi, Prince, c'est moi dont l'utile secours
Vous eût du Labyrinthe enseigné les détours.
Que de soins m'eût coûté cette tête charmante !
Un fil n'eût point assez rassuré votre amante.
Compagne du péril qu'il vous fallait chercher,
660 Moi-même devant vous j'aurais voulu marcher,
Et Phèdre au Labyrinthe avec vous descendue,
Se serait avec vous retrouvée, ou perdue.

    HIPPOLYTE

Dieux ! qu'est-ce que j'entends ? Madame, oubliez-vous
Que Thésée est mon père, et qu'il est votre époux ?

    PHÈDRE

Et sur quoi jugez-vous que j'en perds la mémoire,
Prince ? Aurais-je perdu tout le soin de ma gloire ?

    HIPPOLYTE

Madame, pardonnez. J'avoue en rougissant,
Que j'accusais à tort un discours innocent.
Ma honte ne peut plus soutenir votre vue.
670 Et je vais . . .

    PHÈDRE

                Ah ! cruel, tu m'as trop entendue.
Je t'en ai dit assez pour te tirer d'erreur.
Hé bien, connais donc Phèdre et toute sa fureur.
J'aime. Ne pense pas qu'au moment que je t'aime,
Innocente à mes yeux je m'approuve moi-même,
Ni que du fol amour qui trouble ma raison
Ma lâche complaisance ait nourri le poison.
Objet infortuné des vengeances célestes,
Je m'abhorre encor plus que tu ne me détestes.
Les Dieux m'en sont témoins, ces Dieux qui dans mon flanc

You would have slain the terror of the island,
The monster lapped in labyrinthine wiles;
Into your hand my sister would have thrust,
To unweave those riddling and deceitful ways,
The thread of life and death. But no, she would not—
660 Love would have found a readier wit in me,
And I, Prince, I, devoted and assured,
Could have resolved the devious Labyrinth;
What would I not have done for that sweet head?
How should a thread content your fearful lover?
Half-claimant in the peril that you claimed
I would have walked before you in the way,
And Phaedra, steadfast in the Labyrinth,
Would have returned again with you, or else
Fallen with you.

HIPPOLYTUS

                  Great Gods, what have you said?
670 My lady, can it be that you forget
That you are Theseus' wife, and I his son?

PHAEDRA

And why do you suppose I had forgotten,
Prince? Do I appear so careless of my honour?

HIPPOLYTUS

Forgive, my lady. I own, I blush to own
How blameless are the words that I reproved.
My shame can face it out no more before you,
So let me go . . .

PHAEDRA

               Ah, leave your heartless lying.
You understand and you have heard enough.
Very well then, you shall learn what Phaedra is
680 And all her frenzy. Yes: I am in love.
But never think that even while I love you
I can absolve myself, or hide my face
From my own guiltiness. And never think
The wanton love that blurs my better mind
Grew with the treachery of my consent.
I, singled out for a celestial vengeance,
Unpitied victim, I abhor myself
More than you hate me. Let the Gods bear witness,
Those Gods that set the fire within my breast,

680 Ont allumé le feu fatal à tout mon sang,
Ces Dieux qui se sont fait une gloire cruelle
De séduire le cœur d'une faible mortelle.
Toi-même en ton esprit rappelle le passé.
C'est peu de t'avoir fui, cruel, je t'ai chassé.
J'ai voulu te paraître odieuse, inhumaine.
Pour mieux te résister, j'ai recherché ta haine.
De quoi m'ont profité mes inutiles soins ?
Tu me haïssais plus, je ne t'aimais pas moins.
Tes malheurs te prêtaient encor de nouveaux charmes.
690 J'ai langui, j'ai séché, dans les feux, dans les larmes.
Il suffit de tes yeux pour t'en persuader,
Si tes yeux un moment pouvaient me regarder.
Que dis-je ? Cet aveu que je te viens de faire,
Cet aveu si honteux, le crois-tu volontaire ?
Tremblante pour un fils que je n'osais trahir,
Je te venais prier de ne le point haïr.
Faibles projets d'un cœur trop plein de ce qu'il aime !
Hélas ! je ne t'ai pu parler que de toi-même.
Venge-toi, punis-moi d'un odieux amour.
700 Digne fils du héros qui t'a donné le jour,
Délivre l'univers d'un Monstre qui t'irrite.
La veuve de Thésée ose aimer Hippolyte ?
Crois-moi, ce Monstre affreux ne doit point t'échapper.
Voilà mon cœur. C'est là que ta main doit frapper.
Impatient déjà d'expier son offense
Au-devant de ton bras je le sens qui s'avance.
Frappe. Ou si tu le crois indigne de tes coups,
Si ta haine m'envie un supplice si doux,
Ou si d'un sang trop vil ta main serait trempée,
710 Au défaut de ton bras prête-moi ton épée.
Donne.

ŒNONE

Que faites-vous, Madame ? Justes Dieux !
Mais on vient. Évitez des témoins odieux,
Venez, rentrez, fuyez une honte certaine.

690 The fatal fire of my accursed line;
Those Gods whose majesty and might exulted
In the beguiling of a mortal's weakness.
Turn back the past yourself: how I have laboured
To seem malignant, savage, how I fostered
Your hatred as my ally in the fight.
Did I escape you? No, I banished you.
What fruit repaid these unavailing cares?
You loathed me more, I could not love you less;
Your suffering doubled the spell that binds me,
700 The withering ravage of my flames, my tears.
Your eyes can testify that this is true—
If for one moment they could bear my sight.
Why, this confession of my bitter secret,
My shameful secret, do you think that I
Have made it willingly? I came in fear
For one defenceless that I dare not fail:
I came to pray you not to hate my child.
Precarious resolution of a mind
Too full of what it loves! I came, and spoke
710 Of nothing but yourself.—So now, do justice.
Punish me for this execrable passion.
Approve yourself a hero's son indeed
And sweep this monster from the universe.
Dare Theseus' widow love Hippolytus?
Truly so vile a monster must not live.
My heart is here, and here is where you strike.
Eager to make atonement for its fault
I feel it swell and bound to meet your hand:
Strike. Or am I unworthy of your steel,
720 Or will your hate refuse so sweet a doom,
Or would ignoble blood sully your fingers?
Then hold your hand and let me have your sword.
Give me it.

OENONE

        Stop, my lady. Heavenly powers!
What would you do? But somebody is coming:
Escape their sight, be quick, come back, or face
Inevitable shame.

Exeunt PHAEDRA & OENONE.

SCÈNE VI

HIPPOLYTE, THÉRAMÈNE

THÉRAMÈNE

Est-ce Phèdre qui fuit, ou plutôt qu'on entraîne ?
Pourquoi, Seigneur, pourquoi ces marques de douleur ?
Je vous vois sans épée, interdit, sans couleur ?

HIPPOLYTE

Théramène, fuyons. Ma surprise est extrême.
Je ne puis sans horreur me regarder moi-même.
Phèdre . . . Mais non, grands Dieux ! Qu'en un profond oubli
720   Cet horrible secret demeure enseveli.

THÉRAMÈNE

Si vous voulez partir, la voile est préparée.
Mais Athènes, Seigneur, s'est déjà déclarée.
Ses chefs ont pris les voix de toutes ses tribus.
Votre frère l'emporte, et Phèdre a le dessus.

HIPPOLYTE

Phèdre ?

THÉRAMÈNE

          Un héraut chargé des volontés d'Athènes
De l'État en ses mains vient remettre les rênes.
Son fils est Roi, Seigneur.

HIPPOLYTE

                 Dieux, qui la connaissez,
Est-ce donc sa vertu que vous récompensez ?

THÉRAMÈNE

Cependant un bruit sourd veut que le Roi respire.
730   On prétend que Thésée a paru dans l'Épire.
Mais moi qui l'y cherchai, Seigneur, je sais trop bien . . .

HIPPOLYTE

N'importe, écoutons tout, et ne négligeons rien.
Examinons ce bruit, remontons à sa source.
S'il ne mérite pas d'interrompre ma course,
Partons, et quelque prix qu'il en puisse coûter,
Mettons le sceptre aux mains dignes de le porter.

Fin du second Acte

Enter THERAMENES

THERAMENES
                         Was that the Queen
Half dragged, half rushing out? What, my lord, what
Are all these marks of grief? You stand disarmed,
Dumb, pale . . .
    HIPPOLYTUS
                         Come, let us go, Theramenes.
730 I cannot think of what I have heard and witnessed;
I cannot see myself without disgust.
Phaedra. . . . No more, great Gods! Oblivion
Must shroud away that secret with its shame.
    THERAMENES
If you would leave, my lord, the sail hangs ready;
But Athens is beforehand with her answer:
Her chiefs have counted votes among the tribes;
Your brother has their suffrage, Phaedra wins.
    HIPPOLYTUS
Phaedra!
    THERAMENES
                    A herald of the will of Athens
Will bring the reins of state into her hands.
740 Her son is King.
    HIPPOLYTUS
                         Ye Gods that know her heart,
Is it her righteousness you would repay?
    THERAMENES
And now dark rumours speak again of Theseus:
Some tell that men have seen him in Epirus
Alive; though I, who went to seek him there,
I know full well, my lord . . .
    HIPPOLYTUS
                                   It may be so.
But I would hear whatever rumour tells,
Consult this public cry, divine its sources.
If it be worthless to delay our journey
Then forward! Cost the venture what it will
750 I'll save the sceptre for a worthy hand.

PHÈDRE

Ah! que l'on porte ailleurs les honneurs qu'on m'envoie.
Importune, peux-tu souhaiter qu'on me voie?
De quoi viens-tu flatter mon esprit désolé?
740 Cache-moi bien plutôt, je n'ai que trop parlé.
Mes fureurs au dehors ont osé se répandre.
J'ai dit ce que jamais on ne devait entendre.
Ciel! Comme il m'écoutait! Par combien de détours
L'insensible a longtemps éludé mes discours!
Comme il ne respirait qu'une retraite prompte!
Et combien sa rougeur a redoublé ma honte!
Pourquoi détournais-tu mon funeste dessein?
Hélas! Quand son épée allait chercher mon sein,
A-t-il pâli pour moi? Me l'a-t-il arrachée?
750 Il suffit que ma main l'ait une fois touchée,
Je l'ai rendue horrible à ses yeux inhumains.
Et ce fer malheureux profanerait ses mains.

ŒNONE

Ainsi, dans vos malheurs ne songeant qu'à vous plaindre,
Vous nourrissez un feu, qu'il vous faudrait éteindre.
Ne vaudrait-il pas mieux, digne sang de Minos,
Dans de plus nobles soins chercher votre repos,
Contre un ingrat qui plaît recourir à la fuite,
Régner, et de l'État embrasser la conduite?

PHÈDRE

Moi régner! Moi ranger un État sous ma loi!
760 Quand ma faible raison ne règne plus sur moi,

Act Three

PHAEDRA

Send them away, these heralds and these honours.
Have they a balm to ease a tortured mind?
Be kind: is Phaedra fit for public show?
Rather conceal me, for my secret's out:
Intemperate desire has seen the light,
And what these lips had never thought to utter
He heard. Immortal Gods! and how he listened,
How long he parried, how deviously he turned
To baffle the approaches of my speech!
760 How visibly he yearned to leave my presence!
How painfully his blush revived my shame!
Why did you disappoint me of my death?
Ah, when his weapon pointed at my breast
Did he blench? Did he stir to snatch it back?
Enough for him my fingers at the hilt
And in his heartless reckoning it was vile,
Profaned, a blade that would defile his hand.

OENONE

And so complaining, dwelling on your sorrow,
You feed a fire that wisdom would have quenched.
770 Should not a worthy child of Minos' blood
Look for serenity in nobler tasks,
Fly from a struggle that you cannot win,
Learn to assume the guidance of a kingdom
And be a Queen?

PHAEDRA

             Queen, I? And hold command,
When my own senses rage in mutiny,

Lorsque j'ai de mes sens abandonné l'empire,
Quand sous un joug honteux à peine je respire,
Quand je me meurs.

ŒNONE

Fuyez.

PHÈDRE

Je ne le puis quitter.

ŒNONE

Vous l'osâtes bannir, vous n'osez l'éviter.

PHÈDRE

Il n'est plus temps. Il sait mes ardeurs insensées.
De l'austère pudeur les bornes sont passées.
J'ai déclaré ma honte aux yeux de mon vainqueur,
Et l'espoir malgré moi s'est glissé dans mon cœur.
Toi-même rappelant ma force défaillante,
770 Et mon âme déjà sur mes lèvres errante,
Par tes conseils flatteurs tu m'as su ranimer.
Tu m'as fait entrevoir que je pouvais l'aimer.

ŒNONE

Hélas! de vos malheurs innocente ou coupable,
De quoi pour vous sauver n'étais-je point capable?
Mais si jamais l'offense irrita vos esprits,
Pouvez-vous d'un superbe oublier les mépris?
Avec quels yeux cruels sa rigueur obstinée
Vous laissait à ses pieds peu s'en faut prosternée!
Que son farouche orgueil le rendait odieux!
780 Que Phèdre en ce moment n'avait-elle mes yeux!

PHÈDRE

Œnone, il peut quitter cet orgueil qui te blesse.
Nourri dans les forêts, il en a la rudesse.
Hippolyte endurci par de sauvages lois
Entend parler d'amour pour la première fois.
Peut-être sa surprise a causé son silence,
Et nos plaintes peut-être ont trop de violence.

ŒNONE

Songez qu'une barbare en son sein l'a formé.

PHÈDRE

Quoique Scythe et barbare, elle a pourtant aimé.

ŒNONE

Il a pour tout le sexe une haine fatale.

When in my soul wisdom has lost dominion,
When shame and slavery have bowed my head,
And death is waiting?

OENONE

Fly.

PHAEDRA

I cannot leave him.

OENONE

You drove him away, and cannot go yourself?

PHAEDRA

780 I cannot now. He has seen my raging soul,
Seen me transgress the rigid pale of virtue;
Before those stony eyes I have poured out
My shame, and now, unbidden, secret hope
Has slipped into my breast. Ay, you yourself,
Rallying the wasted forces of my life,
The parting spirit ready on my lips,
Wooed me from death with false and soothing words;
You half persuaded me that I might love.

OENONE

Ah, call me guilty, or call me innocent,
790 I would do worse if anything could save you.
But, if resentment ever stung your mind,
Can you forget the blow of his rebuff,
The insolence, the icy cruelty
That eyed you all but prostrate at his feet,
The arrogant disdain?—how odious
Had Phaedra only seen him as I saw!

PHAEDRA

What if he lost this arrogance, Oenone?
He has the harshness of his forest ways,
And in his hardy life Hippolytus
800 Has never heard of love until to-day.
What if surprise had robbed him of his speech?
What if we blamed him more than he deserved?

OENONE

He was conceived in a Barbarian's womb.

PHAEDRA

Barbarian, Scythian, still she learned to love.

OENONE

He hates our sex with firm and deadly hate.

PHÈDRE

790 Je ne me verrai point préférer de rivale.
Enfin, tous tes conseils ne sont plus de saison.
Sers ma fureur, Œnone, et non point ma raison.
Il oppose à l'amour un cœur inaccessible.
Cherchons pour l'attaquer quelque endroit plus sensible.
Les charmes d'un empire ont paru le toucher.
Athènes l'attirait, il n'a pu s'en cacher.
Déjà de ses vaisseaux la pointe était tournée,
Et la voile flottait aux vents abandonnée.
Va trouver de ma part ce jeune ambitieux,
800 Œnone. Fais briller la couronne à ses yeux.
Qu'il mette sur son front le sacré diadème.
Je ne veux que l'honneur de l'attacher moi-même.
Cédons-lui ce pouvoir que je ne puis garder.
Il instruira mon fils dans l'art de commander.
Peut-être il voudra bien lui tenir lieu de père.
Je mets sous son pouvoir et le fils et la mère.
Pour le fléchir enfin tente tous les moyens.
Tes discours trouveront plus d'accès que les miens.
Presse, pleure, gémis, plains-lui Phèdre mourante.
810 Ne rougis point de prendre une voix suppliante.
Je t'avoûrai de tout, je n'espère qu'en toi.
Va, j'attends ton retour pour disposer de moi.

SCÈNE II
PHÈDRE *seule*

O toi! qui vois la honte où je suis descendue,
Implacable Vénus, suis-je assez confondue?
Tu ne saurais plus loin pousser ta cruauté.
Ton triomphe est parfait, tous tes traits ont porté.
Cruelle, si tu veux une gloire nouvelle,
Attaque un ennemi qui te soit plus rebelle.
Hippolyte te fuit, et bravant ton courroux,
820 Jamais à tes autels n'a fléchi les genoux.
Ton nom semble offenser ses superbes oreilles.
Déesse, venge-toi, nos causes sont pareilles.
Qu'il aime. Mais déjà tu reviens sur tes pas,
Œnone? On me déteste, on ne t'écoute pas.

PHAEDRA

So I shall never fear another woman.
Enough: such counsels had their season once;
My passion now commands you, and not my reason.
Though hard and inaccessible to love,
810 Another side lies weaker to attack—
The sweets of empire tempted him, I think;
Athens allured him more than he could hide.
His ships already turned their prows to sea
With canvas rigged and offered to the breeze.
Find him, Oenone, find this ambitious boy,
Show him the glitter of the Athenian crown,
Bid him assume the diadem and the glory;
I only ask to lay it on his brow.
Into his hand descends authority
820 I cannot grasp, and he shall teach my son
The science of command—even he might
Look as a father on him. In his power
I now resign the orphan and the mother.
Incline his heart by any means you know,
Use—do not blush—the voice of supplication,
I sanction all. I have no other hope;
Go, till you come again I cannot tell
What else I have to do. *Exit* OENONE

PHAEDRA *alone*

O Thou, that knowest
How deep in shame my soul is overwhelmed,
830 Venus, O Venus unappeasable,
This is the consummation of thy hatred.
These must be the limits of thy cruelty.
Thy triumph is entire, each shot has told.
Art thou not sated yet with victory?
Find tougher quarry then: Hippolytus
Rejects thy deity, derides thy wrath,
He never bent the knee before thy altar;
Thy name seems hideous in his stubborn ears.
Goddess, avenge; and vengeance will be mine!
840 Teach him to love . . . Oenone, here so soon?
I am rejected then, you were not heard.

SCÈNE III
PHÈDRE, ŒNONE

ŒNONE
Il faut d'un vain amour étouffer la pensée,
Madame. Rappelez votre vertu passée.
Le Roi, qu'on a cru mort, va paraître à vos yeux,
Thésée est arrivé. Thésée est en ces lieux.
Le peuple, pour le voir, court et se précipite.
830 Je sortais par votre ordre, et cherchais Hippolyte,
Lorsque jusques au ciel mille cris élancés . . .
PHÈDRE
Mon époux est vivant, Œnone, c'est assez.
J'ai fait l'indigne aveu d'un amour qui l'outrage,
Il vit. Je ne veux pas en savoir davantage.
ŒNONE
Quoi ?
PHÈDRE
              Je te l'ai prédit, mais tu n'as pas voulu.
Sur mes justes remords tes pleurs ont prévalu.
Je mourais ce matin digne d'être pleurée.
J'ai suivi tes conseils, je meurs déshonorée.
ŒNONE
Vous mourez ?
PHÈDRE
                        Juste Ciel ! Qu'ai-je fait aujourd'hui ?
840 Mon époux va paraître, et son fils avec lui.
Je verrai le témoin de ma flamme adultère
Observer de quel front j'ose aborder son père,
Le cœur gros de soupirs, qu'il n'a point écoutés,
L'œil humide de pleurs, par l'ingrat rebutés.
Penses-tu que sensible à l'honneur de Thésée,
Il lui cache l'ardeur dont je suis embrasée ?
Laissera-t-il trahir et son père et son Roi ?
Pourra-t-il contenir l'horreur qu'il a pour moi ?
Il se tairait en vain. Je sais mes perfidies,
850 Œnone, et ne suis point de ces femmes hardies,
Qui goûtant dans le crime une tranquille paix
Ont su se faire un front qui ne rougit jamais.
Je connais mes fureurs, je les rappelle toutes.

Enter OENONE

OENONE
Stifle the memory of a hopeless passion,
My lady; summon up your earlier virtue.
The King's not dead, and you will see him soon.
Theseus has landed. He is coming here.
The populace are rushing to salute him,
And as I passed obedient to your mission
Unending cheers rose up on every hand—

PHAEDRA
He is not dead. Nothing else signifies,
850 Oenone. I revealed a lawless love
That wounds him in his honour. And he lives.
What needs there more?

OENONE
But yet—

PHAEDRA
I told you so;
And you would not. Foreboding and remorse
Have yielded to your tears. Only this morning
My death was not unworthy to be pitied:
I took your counsel, and I die disgraced.

OENONE
Die?

PHAEDRA
Righteous Gods! The things this day has seen!
And now, as I meet my husband and his son
I know this witness of adulterous passion
860 Studies my countenance before his father—
My heart heavy with sighs he would not hear,
My eyelids drenched with tears that he despised.
Do you think his tenderness for Theseus' honour
Would hide away the memory of my falsehood,
My treason to a father and a King?
Will he repress the loathing I inspire?
What if he did? I know my treachery,
Oenone. And if there are intrepid women
Who taste a flawless quietude in crime
870 And force their countenance to show no shame,
I am not such. My misdeeds rise before me;

Il me semble déjà que ces murs, que ces voûtes
Vont prendre la parole, et prêts à m'accuser
Attendent mon époux, pour le désabuser.
Mourons. De tant d'horreurs qu'un trépas me délivre.
Est-ce un malheur si grand que de cesser de vivre ?
La mort aux malheureux ne cause point d'effroi.
860 Je ne crains que le nom que je laisse après moi.
Pour mes tristes enfants quel affreux héritage !
Le sang de Jupiter doit enfler leur courage.
Mais quelque juste orgueil qu'inspire un sang si beau,
Le crime d'une mère est un pesant fardeau.
Je tremble qu'un discours hélas ! trop véritable
Un jour ne leur reproche une mère coupable.
Je tremble qu'opprimés de ce poids odieux
L'un ni l'autre jamais n'ose lever les yeux.

ŒNONE

Il n'en faut point douter, je les plains l'un et l'autre.
870 Jamais crainte ne fut plus juste que la vôtre.
Mais à de tels affronts pourquoi les exposer ?
Pourquoi contre vous-même allez-vous déposer ?
C'en est fait. On dira que Phèdre trop coupable
De son époux trahi fuit l'aspect redoutable.
Hippolyte est heureux qu'aux dépens de vos jours
Vous-même en expirant appuyez ses discours.
A votre accusateur que pourrai-je répondre ?
Je serai devant lui trop facile à confondre.
De son triomphe affreux je le verrai jouir,
880 Et conter votre honte à qui voudra l'ouïr.
Ah ! que plutôt du Ciel la flamme me dévore !
Mais ne me trompez point, vous est-il cher encore ?
De quel œil voyez-vous ce Prince audacieux ?

PHÈDRE

Je le vois comme un Monstre effroyable à mes yeux.

ŒNONE

Pourquoi donc lui céder une victoire entière ?
Vous le craignez. Osez l'accuser la première
Du crime dont il peut vous charger aujourd'hui.
Qui vous démentira ? Tout parle contre lui.

And even now these over-arching walls
Seem full of tongues, impatient to accuse me
Before my husband, and proclaim his wrong.
Oh for a death, and surcease from my anguish!
Is life so precious and so hard to leave?
Need the tormented hesitate to die?
Only I fear the name I leave behind—
The legacy of horror for my children,
880 Whose blood, the very blood of Jupiter,
Should swell their hearts with pride: now they must lift
The burden of a mother's infamy.
My soul foretells that malice, soon or late,
Will throw my black reproach into their faces,
And crushed so cruelly they may never dare
To look with level eyes upon their kind.

OENONE

It is most true. They both are to be pitied,
And never sorrow was foretold more surely.
But why abandon them to the ordeal?
890 Why be the witness that betrays your cause?
For all is lost; and all the world will judge
That Phaedra knows her guilt, and dare not wait
The awful presence of an outraged husband.
Hippolytus should thank you for a deed
Stronger than all his words on his behalf;
And what can I respond to your accuser?
Confounded, tongue-tied, I must live to see
Him taste a hideous triumph undisturbed
And chronicle your shame to all mankind.
900 May fire from Heaven fall upon me sooner!
But tell me this, and tell without dissembling:
Do you still love him, this presumptuous Prince?
How does he now appear . . . ?

PHAEDRA

                                    I see him now
Grim as a monster and as terrible.

OENONE

Then why concede him victory unresisted?
Do you fear him? Attack before he strikes
And use the imputation he prepares
For you. What can refute you? Every sign

Son épée en vos mains heureusement laissée,
890 Votre trouble présent, votre douleur passée,
Son père par vos cris dès longtemps prévenu,
Et déjà son exil par vous-même obtenu.

PHÈDRE

Moi, que j'ose opprimer et noircir l'innocence !

ŒNONE

Mon zèle n'a besoin que de votre silence.
Tremblante comme vous j'en sens quelque remords.
Vous me verriez plus prompte affronter mille morts.
Mais puisque je vous perds sans ce triste remède,
Votre vie est pour moi d'un prix à qui tout cède.
Je parlerai. Thésée aigri par mes avis
900 Bornera sa vengeance à l'exil de son fils.
Un père en punissant, Madame, est toujours père.
Un supplice léger suffit à sa colère.
Mais le sang innocent dût-il être versé,
Que ne demande point votre honneur menacé ?
C'est un trésor trop cher pour oser le commettre.
Quelque loi qu'il vous dicte il faut vous y soumettre,
Madame, et pour sauver notre Honneur combattu,
Il faut immoler tout, et même la Vertu.
On vient, je vois Thésée.

PHÈDRE

                                    Ah ! je vois Hippolyte.
910 Dans ses yeux insolents je vois ma perte écrite.
Fais ce que tu voudras, je m'abandonne à toi.
Dans le trouble où je suis je ne puis rien pour moi.

SCÈNE IV
THÉSÉE, HIPPOLYTE, PHÈDRE, ŒNONE, THÉRAMÈNE

THÉSÉE

La fortune à mes vœux cesse d'être opposée,
Madame, et dans vos bras met . . .

PHÈDRE

                                    Arrêtez, Thésée,
Et ne profanez point des transports si charmants.
Je ne mérite plus ces doux empressements.
Vous êtes offensé. La fortune jalouse

Informs against him—first his sword that Fortune
910 Leaves in your hands, and then this day's distress,
And those disconsolate months of misery,
And long ago his father's mind prepared
When long ago you claimed his banishment.

PHAEDRA

Shall I defame and murder innocence?

OENONE

Lend me but silence and my zeal suffices.
Like you I shudder at my remedy
And dread it deeper than a thousand deaths.
But either this, or else I lose my mistress,
And in your loss all other values fade.
920 So I will speak. Theseus will rage, but still
He'll take no more revenge than banishment.
A father punishing is still a father
Whose love is louder than the voice of justice;
But guiltless blood is nothing in the scales
Against the imperilled honour of your name.
That is a jewel far too dear to hazard;
It is a law we dare not disobey;
And when our honour stands at such a cost
Virtue itself must go for sacrifice.
930 —Here they are. I see Theseus.

PHAEDRA

                              And I see
Hippolytus, and his unflinching eyes
Spell my dishonour. Do what you will, Oenone.
I am in your hands. In this tormented hour
To save myself is more than I can do.

Enter THESEUS, HIPPOLYTUS, & THERAMENES

THESEUS

Fortune has smiled again, my dearest lady,
And now your sweet embrace—

PHAEDRA

                              No, Theseus; stop,
Do not pollute this love and this delight.
No longer I deserve this tenderness.
You have been wronged. The jealousy of Fortune

N'a pas en votre absence épargné votre épouse.
Indigne de vous plaire, et de vous approcher,
920 Je ne dois désormais songer qu'à me cacher.

SCÈNE V
THÉSÉE, HIPPOLYTE, THÉRAMÈNE

THÉSÉE
Quel est l'étrange accueil qu'on fait à votre père,
Mon fils ?
HIPPOLYTE
                    Phèdre peut seule expliquer ce mystère.
Mais si mes vœux ardents vous peuvent émouvoir,
Permettez-moi, Seigneur, de ne la plus revoir.
Souffrez que pour jamais le tremblant Hippolyte
Disparaisse des lieux que votre épouse habite.
THÉSÉE
Vous, mon fils, me quitter ?
HIPPOLYTE
                                        Je ne la cherchais pas,
C'est vous qui sur ces bords conduisîtes ses pas.
Vous daignâtes, Seigneur, aux rives de Trézène
930 Confier en partant Aricie, et la Reine.
Je fus même chargé du soin de les garder.
Mais quels soins désormais peuvent me retarder ?
Assez dans les forêts mon oisive jeunesse
Sur de vils ennemis a montré son adresse.
Ne pourrai-je, en fuyant un indigne repos,
D'un sang plus glorieux teindre mes javelots ?
Vous n'aviez pas encore atteint l'âge où je touche,
Déjà plus d'un Tyran, plus d'un Monstre farouche
Avait de votre bras senti la pesanteur.
940 Déjà de l'insolence heureux persécuteur
Vous aviez des deux mers assuré les rivages.
Le libre voyageur ne craignait plus d'outrages.
Hercule respirant sur le bruit de vos coups
Déjà de son travail se reposait sur vous.
Et moi, fils inconnu d'un si glorieux père,
Je suis même encor loin des traces de ma mère.
Souffrez que mon courage ose enfin s'occuper.
Souffrez, si quelque Monstre a pu vous échapper,

940 Has not respected her you left behind you;
     And now, unworthy to approach your love,
     My sole desire must be for solitude.
     Exit

          THESEUS
     What is this cheerless welcome that I find here,
     My son?
          HIPPOLYTUS
               A riddle Phaedra must interpret,
     No one else can. But now if prayers can move
     I ask but this, my lord, never to see
     Her face again, but to live out my life
     Safe, far away, forgotten by the Queen.
          THESEUS
     And now my son forsakes me!
          HIPPOLYTUS
                              For you know
950 I never sought her, but you brought her here
     At your departure; and the coasts of Trozen
     Became the dwelling of Aricia
     And of the Queen. I was to be their guardian.
     But now what duty keeps me from my life?
     Inglorious victories among the forests
     Weary my idle youth, my wasted skill.
     I long to waken from obscurity
     And dip my hunter's spear in a nobler red.
     Before you had spent the years that I have counted
960 What robbers, what oppressors, and what monsters
     Had known the weight of that revengeful arm
     Victor and scourge of wanton insolence!
     While on the quiet shores of either sea
     The traveller learnt to take his road in peace;
     Hercules heard your prowess and drew breath,
     Leaving his triumphs and his toils to you—
     And I, the unknown son of such a father,
     Have much to do to reach my mother's footsteps.
     Now let my unfledged valour learn to dare;
970 Let me, if anywhere some monster yet

Que j'apporte à vos pieds sa dépouille honorable ;
950 Ou que d'un beau trépas la mémoire durable
Eternisant des jours si noblement finis,
Prouve à tout l'avenir que j'étais votre fils.

THÉSÉE

Que vois-je ? Quelle horreur dans ces lieux répandue
Fait fuir devant mes yeux ma famille éperdue ?
Si je reviens si craint, et si peu désiré,
O Ciel ! de ma prison pourquoi m'as-tu tiré ?
Je n'avais qu'un ami. Son imprudente flamme
Du Tyran de l'Épire allait ravir la femme.
Je servais à regret ses desseins amoureux.
960 Mais le sort irrité nous aveuglait tous deux.
Le Tyran m'a surpris sans défense et sans armes.
J'ai vu Pirithoüs, triste objet de mes larmes,
Livré par ce barbare à des monstres cruels,
Qu'il nourrissait du sang des malheureux mortels.
Moi-même il m'enferma dans des cavernes sombres,
Lieux profonds, et voisins de l'Empire des Ombres.
Les Dieux après six mois enfin m'ont regardé.
J'ai su tromper les yeux de qui j'étais gardé.
D'un perfide ennemi j'ai purgé la Nature.
970 A ses monstres lui-même a servi de pâture.
Et lorsque avec transport je pense m'approcher
De tout ce que les Dieux m'ont laissé de plus cher ;
Que dis-je ? Quand mon âme à soi-même rendue
Vient se rassasier d'une si chère vue ;
Je n'ai pour tout accueil que des frémissements.
Tout fuit, tout se refuse à mes embrassements.
Et moi-même éprouvant la terreur que j'inspire,
Je voudrais être encor dans les prisons d'Épire.
Parlez. Phèdre se plaint que je suis outragé.
980 Qui m'a trahi ? Pourquoi ne suis-je pas vengé ?
La Grèce, à qui mon bras fut tant de fois utile,
A-t-elle au criminel accordé quelque asile ?
Vous ne répondez point. Mon fils, mon propre fils
Est-il d'intelligence avec mes ennemis ?
Entrons. C'est trop garder un doute qui m'accable.
Connaissons à la fois le crime et le coupable.
Que Phèdre explique enfin le trouble où je la voi.

Escapes you, drag its trophy to your feet,
Or by the record of a glorious failure
Find life for ever in a fitting death
And show posterity I was your son.

THESEUS

What is it? What invading blast of fear
Empties my very home at my approach?
Why, O ye Gods, to face these shrinking looks,
This lack of love, did ye deliver me?
I had one friend. His unregarding passion
980 Conspired to carry back from far Epirus
The tyrant's Queen. I helped, against my will,
But Fate was pitiless, and we were blind.
The villain caught me all unarmed, unwatching,
And these two eyes—that weep him yet—beheld
Pirithous under the fangs of beasts
Fatted on human slaughter; and I spent
Deep in the sightless silence of his dungeons
Down near the horrible empire of the Dead,
Six months. Then Heaven thought on me again.
990 I tricked the watchful eyes. I purged creation
Of one perfidious enemy, and his blood
Glutted his own fell monsters. Now at length
Free, and restored to all that's left to love,
Now that my soul aspires to nothing more
Than the enjoyment of their blessed sight,
Grief and lament is all my salutation,
None will abide to suffer my embraces;
And, chilled by the contagion of the fears
That breathe about my path, I'd rather be
1000 A prisoner again and in Epirus.

Speak out. Phaedra declares I've been betrayed.
Who wronged me? Why is not the wrong avenged?
Has Greece, so long beholden to this arm,
Offered a refuge to the criminal?
—You will not answer? Is my son, my son,
A shield and ally of my enemies?
I will go in, for this suspense unmans me.
I will find out the culprit and the offence.
Phaedra must tell me what her sorrow is.
Exit

SCÈNE VI
HIPPOLYTE, THÉRAMÈNE

HIPPOLYTE

Où tendait ce discours qui m'a glacé d'effroi ?
Phèdre toujours en proie à sa fureur extrême
990 Veut-elle s'accuser et se perdre elle-même ?
Dieux ! que dira le Roi ? Quel funeste poison
L'amour a répandu sur toute sa maison !
Moi-même plein d'un feu que sa haine réprouve,
Quel il m'a vu jadis, et quel il me retrouve !
De noirs pressentiments viennent m'épouvanter.
Mais l'innocence enfin n'a rien à redouter.
Allons, cherchons ailleurs par quelle heureuse adresse
Je pourrai de mon père émouvoir la tendresse,
Et lui dire un amour qu'il peut vouloir troubler,
1000 Mais que tout son pouvoir ne saurait ébranler.

Fin du troisième Acte

HIPPOLYTUS

1010 What did her words portend? They froze my blood.
Would Phaedra in her ecstasy of frenzy
Denounce her guilt and give her case away?
Gods, when the King is told! Death-dealing Love,
What blighting mists thou hast wrapped around his house!
And I with my secret of disloyal passion,
What was I once, what will he think me now!
My mind is dark with unaccomplished shapes
Of evil: but should innocence be afraid?
I must look for better times and better ways
1020 To move my father's heart, and then reveal
Love he may doom to parting and to tears
But fixed beyond his force to overthrow.

Acte IV

THÉSÉE

Ah! Qu'est-ce que j'entends? Un traître, un téméraire
Préparait cet outrage à l'honneur de son père?
Avec quelle rigueur, Destin, tu me poursuis!
Je ne sais où je vais, je ne sais où je suis.
O tendresse! O bonté trop mal récompensée!
Projet audacieux! Détestable pensée!
Pour parvenir au but de ses noires amours,
L'insolent de la force empruntait le secours.
J'ai reconnu le fer, instrument de sa rage,
1010 Ce fer dont je l'armai pour un plus noble usage.
Tous les liens du sang n'ont pu le retenir!
Et Phèdre différait à le faire punir!
Le silence de Phèdre épargnait le coupable!

ŒNONE

Phèdre épargnait plutôt un père déplorable.
Honteuse du dessein d'un amant furieux,
Et du feu criminel qu'il a pris dans ses yeux,
Phèdre mourait, Seigneur, et sa main meurtrière
Éteignait de ses yeux l'innocente lumière.
J'ai vu lever le bras, j'ai couru la sauver.
1020 Moi seule à votre amour j'ai su la conserver;
Et plaignant à la fois son trouble et vos alarmes,
J'ai servi malgré moi d'interprète à ses larmes.

THÉSÉE

Le perfide! Il n'a pu s'empêcher de pâlir.
De crainte en m'abordant je l'ai vu tressaillir.
Je me suis étonné de son peu d'allégresse.
Ses froids embrassements ont glacé ma tendresse.

Act Four

THESEUS, OENONE

THESEUS
Ah! What have you said? The rebel, the betrayer
Conceived this outrage on his father's honour?
How unrelenting is thy hand upon me,
O Destiny! I know not where I go,
I know not what I do. All my long kindness
Wasted, paid with this hideous wanton plot!
And with the argument and threat of steel
1030 To enforce his dark design! I know that sword,
I gave it him, I strapped it to his side—
For nobler work than this. Not all the bonds
Of blood itself could hold him back; and she
Could hesitate to punish, and her silence
Showed mercy to the wrongdoer!

OENONE

Say rather
Showed mercy to a father's suffering.
Shamed by a lover's frenzy, and ashamed
That her chaste eyes could kindle such a fire,
She would have died, my lord, and dimmed for ever
1040 Herself the innocent lustre of those eyes.
The arm was raised. I hastened, I preserved
Her life for the embraces of her lord,
And pitying your fears and her confusion
Became the unwilling spokesman of her tears.

THESEUS
The perfidy! Yes, for all his craft, he paled;
He quaked with fear, I saw it as he came;
I marvelled then to feel his joylessness
And froze against the chill of his embrace.

Mais ce coupable amour dont il est dévoré,
Dans Athènes déjà s'était-il déclaré ?

ŒNONE

Seigneur, souvenez-vous des plaintes de la Reine.
1030 Un amour criminel causa toute sa haine.

THÉSÉE

Et ce feu dans Trézène a donc recommencé ?

ŒNONE

Je vous ai dit, Seigneur, tout ce qui s'est passé.
C'est trop laisser la Reine à sa douleur mortelle.
Souffrez que je vous quitte et me range auprès d'elle.

SCÈNE II
THÉSÉE, HIPPOLYTE

THÉSÉE

Ah ! le voici, grands Dieux ! A ce noble maintien
Quel œil ne serait pas trompé comme le mien ?
Faut-il que sur le front d'un profane adultère
Brille de la vertu le sacré caractère ?
Et ne devrait-on pas à des signes certains
1040 Reconnaître le cœur des perfides humains ?

HIPPOLYTE

Puis-je vous demander quel funeste nuage,
Seigneur, a pu troubler votre auguste visage ?
N'osez-vous confier ce secret à ma foi ?

THÉSÉE

Perfide, oses-tu bien te montrer devant moi ?
Monstre, qu'a trop longtemps épargné le tonnerre,
Reste impur des Brigands dont j'ai purgé la terre.
Après que le transport d'un amour plein d'horreur
Jusqu'au lit de ton père a porté sa fureur,
Tu m'oses présenter une tête ennemie,
1050 Tu parais dans des lieux pleins de ton infamie,
Et ne vas pas chercher sous un ciel inconnu
Des pays où mon nom ne soit point parvenu.
Fuis, traître. Ne viens point braver ici ma haine,
Et tenter un courroux que je retiens à peine.
C'est bien assez pour moi de l'opprobre éternel
D'avoir pu mettre au jour un fils si criminel,
Sans que ta mort encor honteuse à ma mémoire
De mes nobles travaux vienne souiller la gloire.

—Did you not say, the love that burns in him
1050 Had shown itself in Athens long before?

OENONE

My lord, remember how the Queen abhorred him;
It was unhallowed love that caused her hatred.

THESEUS

And now, in Trozen, it has flared again?

OENONE

I have told you all, my lord; but I have left
My lady too long now with her deadly sorrow,
And, by your leave, my place is at her side.
Exit.

Enter HIPPOLYTUS

THESEUS

So, here he comes. Great Gods, that noble carriage
Would it not blind another's eye, as mine?
Then sacrilegious and adulterous heads
1060 May flaunt the sacred emblem of the pure?
Why is there no infallible badge to blazon
The minds of our dissembling race of men?

HIPPOLYTUS

May I not know, my lord, why such a weight
Of cloud darkens the majesty of your brow?
Must this be secret from my loyalty?

THESEUS

Dissembler! Dare you come so near to me?
Monster the thunderbolts reprieve too long,
Corrupted straggler of the brigand race
I cleansed the earth of once, how dare you still
1070 Parade that odious face, here where your frenzy
Clutched at a father's bed? How dare you pace
These halls where all things tell of your dishonour?
Why are you not far hence, where skies unknown
Illumine coasts that never knew my name?
Be gone, you traitor. Lingering you taunt too long
A hate, an anger hardly to be stayed.
Enough for me the indelible reproach
Of fathering you, without the soil of murder
To smother my bright deeds from memory.

Fuis. Et si tu ne veux qu'un châtiment soudain
1060 T'ajoute aux scélérats qu'a punis cette main,
Prends garde que jamais l'astre qui nous éclaire
Ne te voie en ces lieux mettre un pied téméraire.
Fuis, dis-je, et sans retour précipitant tes pas,
De ton horrible aspect purge tous mes États.
Et toi, Neptune, et toi, si jadis mon courage
D'infâmes assassins nettoya ton rivage,
Souviens-toi que pour prix de mes efforts heureux
Tu promis d'exaucer le premier de mes vœux.
Dans les longues rigueurs d'une prison cruelle
1070 Je n'ai point imploré ta puissance immortelle.
Avare du secours que j'attends de tes soins
Mes vœux t'ont réservé pour de plus grands besoins.
Je t'implore aujourd'hui. Venge un malheureux père.
J'abandonne ce traître à toute ta colère.
Étouffe dans son sang ses désirs effrontés.
Thésée à tes fureurs connaîtra tes bontés.

HIPPOLYTE

D'un amour criminel Phèdre accuse Hippolyte ?
Un tel excès d'horreur rend mon âme interdite ;
Tant de coups imprévus m'accablent à la fois
1080 Qu'ils m'ôtent la parole, et m'étouffent la voix.

THÉSÉE

Traître, tu prétendais qu'en un lâche silence
Phèdre ensevelirait ta brutale insolence.
Il fallait en fuyant ne pas abandonner
Le fer, qui dans ses mains aide à te condamner.
Ou plutôt il fallait comblant ta perfidie
Lui ravir tout d'un coup la parole et la vie.

HIPPOLYTE

D'un mensonge si noir justement irrité,
Je devrais faire ici parler la Vérité,
Seigneur. Mais je supprime un secret qui vous touche.
1090 Approuvez le respect qui me ferme la bouche ;
Et sans vouloir vous-même augmenter vos ennuis,
Examinez ma vie, et songez qui je suis.
Quelques crimes toujours précèdent les grands crimes.
Quiconque a pu franchir les bornes légitimes
Peut violer enfin les droits les plus sacrés.

1080 —Be gone. And if you would not share the sentence
　　　Of malefactors doomed by this swift hand
　　　Take care that never again the sun that lights us
　　　Finds your rebellious feet upon this shore.
　　　Be gone I tell you, out of my dominions
　　　And cleanse them for ever of your loathsome presence.
　　　　　And now hear, Neptune, hear. If once my courage
　　　Scoured off a scum of bandits from thy coasts
　　　Remember thou hast sworn in recompense
　　　To grant one prayer. In long and stern confinement
1090 I called not thy undying power; I saved thee,
　　　Thrifty of all the aid I hoped for, till
　　　A greater need. To-day I pray: avenge
　　　A mourning father. To thy wrath I entrust
　　　This profligate. Stifle his lust in blood.
　　　Let Theseus read thy kindness in thy rage.

　　　　HIPPOLYTUS

　　　With such a love Hippolytus is charged
　　　By Phaedra! Weight of horror crushes me;
　　　So many assaults unlooked-for, stroke on stroke,
　　　Leave me no words.

　　　　THESEUS

　　　　　　　　　　And so you judged that Phaedra's
1100 Compliant silence would have muffled up
　　　Your savage insolence. You might have waited
　　　To gather up the sword that now, in her hands,
　　　Helps to convict you. Or why not, better still,
　　　Heap up the measure of your infamy
　　　With one good blow to finish breath and life?

　　　　HIPPOLYTUS

　　　In anger at a calumny so monstrous,
　　　My lord, I should speak out, but for a secret
　　　That partly touches you. I beg you sanction
　　　Respect that silences what I might say;
1110 Labour no more to probe into your pain,
　　　Look on my life, consider what I am:
　　　The greatest crimes have lesser crimes before them;
　　　The rest is easy when the way is known;

Ainsi que la Vertu le Crime a ses degrés.
Et jamais on n'a vu la timide Innocence
Passer subitement à l'extrême licence.
Un jour seul ne fait point d'un mortel vertueux
1100 Un perfide assassin, un lâche incestueux.
Élevé dans le sein d'une chaste héroïne
Je n'ai point de son sang démenti l'origine.
Pitthée estimé sage entre tous les humains
Daigna m'instruire encore au sortir de ses mains.
Je ne veux point me peindre avec trop d'avantage;
Mais si quelque vertu m'est tombée en partage,
Seigneur, je crois surtout avoir fait éclater
La haine des forfaits qu'on ose m'imputer.
C'est par là qu'Hippolyte est connu dans la Grèce.
1110 J'ai poussé la vertu jusques à la rudesse.
On sait de mes chagrins l'inflexible rigueur.
Le jour n'est pas plus pur que le fond de mon cœur,
Et l'on veut qu'Hippolyte épris d'un feu profane . . .

    THÉSÉE

Oui, c'est ce même orgueil, lâche, qui te condamne.
Je vois de tes froideurs le principe odieux.
Phèdre seule charmait tes impudiques yeux.
Et pour tout autre objet ton âme indifférente
Dédaignait de brûler d'une flamme innocente.

    HIPPOLYTE

Non, mon père, ce cœur (c'est trop vous le celer)
1120 N'a point d'un chaste amour dédaigné de brûler.
Je confesse à vos pieds ma véritable offense.
J'aime, j'aime, il est vrai, malgré votre défense.
Aricie à ses lois tient mes vœux asservis.
La fille de Pallante a vaincu votre fils.
Je l'adore, et mon âme à vos ordres rebelle
Ne peut ni soupirer ni brûler que pour elle.

    THÉSÉE

Tu l'aimes? Ciel! Mais non, l'artifice est grossier.
Tu te feins criminel pour te justifier.

    HIPPOLYTE

Seigneur, depuis six mois je l'évite, et je l'aime.
1130 Je venais en tremblant vous le dire à vous-même.
Hé quoi? De votre erreur rien ne vous peut tirer?
Par quel affreux serment faut-il vous rassurer?
Que la Terre, le Ciel, que toute la Nature . . .

Like virtue, vice is gradual. No one day
Made any good man vile, murderous, incestuous,
And innocence is slow to dare, and slow
To push beyond the boundaries of law.
I had a mother, as chaste as she was valiant,
Nor have I derogated from her blood;
1120 Pittheus, wise among men, took up my nurture
After her hands. I would not praise myself,
But, if one virtue was allotted mine,
May I not claim, my lord, to loathe that act
My enemies presume to speak of? This
Has made Hippolytus his name in Greece—
Unstudied honour rude in its excess,
Rugged, intractable austerity.
The daylight is no cleaner than the deeps
Of this my heart. What, sacrilegious lust
1130 Could stain Hippolytus?

THESEUS

      And this condemns you:
That was the foul source fed your vaunted coldness—
No other woman's love was worth your interest
Unless it offered pleasures more than lawful.

HIPPOLYTUS

No, father, you shall hear the truth. This heart
Has not refused an honourable yoke.
Here at your feet I will confess—I love,
And love in disobedience to your will.
Aricia's beauty holds my heart enslaved
And Pallas' daughter has subdued your son.
1140 I worship her, forgetful of my duty
And have no room to feel another passion.

THESEUS

You love her! No—a pitiful pretence;
You feign that crime to clear yourself of this.

HIPPOLYTUS

These six months I have hid from love, and loved,
My lord; I came here to confess to you
In trembling. But is it so? Will nothing move you?
What fearful oath will win you to believe?
Witness the Earth, the Heavens, and all Nature . . .

THÉSÉE

Toujours les scélérats ont recours au parjure.
Cesse, cesse, et m'épargne un importun discours,
Si ta fausse vertu n'a point d'autre secours.

HIPPOLYTE

Elle vous paraît fausse, et pleine d'artifice;
Phèdre au fond de son cœur me rend plus de justice.

THÉSÉE

Ah! que ton impudence excite mon courroux!

HIPPOLYTE

1140 Quel temps à mon exil, quel lieu prescrivez-vous?

THÉSÉE

Fusses-tu par delà les Colonnes d'Alcide,
Je me croirais encor trop voisin d'un perfide.

HIPPOLYTE

Chargé du crime affreux dont vous me soupçonnez,
Quels amis me plaindront quand vous m'abandonnez?

THÉSÉE

Va chercher des amis, dont l'estime funeste
Honore l'adultère, applaudisse à l'inceste;
Des traîtres, des ingrats, sans honneur et sans loi,
Dignes de protéger un méchant tel que toi.

HIPPOLYTE

Vous me parlez toujours d'inceste et d'adultère!
1150 Je me tais. Cependant Phèdre sort d'une mère,
Phèdre est d'un sang, Seigneur, vous le savez trop bien,
De toutes ces horreurs plus rempli que le mien.

THÉSÉE

Quoi! ta rage à mes yeux perd toute retenue?
Pour la dernière fois ôte-toi de ma vue.
Sors, traître. N'attends pas qu'un père furieux
Te fasse avec opprobre arracher de ces lieux.

SCÈNE III
THÉSÉE *seul*

Misérable, tu cours à ta perte infaillible.
Neptune par le Fleuve aux Dieux mêmes terrible
M'a donné sa parole, et va l'exécuter.

THESEUS

What felon ever feared a perjury?

1150 Peace, peace. Waste no more time on idle stories
If that fine virtue rests on aids like these.

HIPPOLYTUS

You see it as a mockery, a lie:
But Phaedra in her heart of hearts knows better.

THESEUS

Shall I endure so much effrontery?

HIPPOLYTUS

What place of exile, and how long a time
Do you appoint?

THESEUS

                        Past the Pillars of Hercules
A traitor's presence is too close for me.

HIPPOLYTUS

What friendship shall I find to comfort me
When you have cast me out, dishonoured thus?

THESEUS

1160 Find yourself friends whose dangerous regard
Goes to adultery and honours incest,
Deceivers, ingrates, free of law and shame,
Fit to protect a suppliant like you.

HIPPOLYTUS

And still you taunt me with adultery
And incest. How can I reply? But Phaedra
Came of a mother, Phaedra's is a blood,
My lord, you do not need me to recall it,
More laden with their awful taint than mine.

THESEUS

How dare you go so far before my face?

1170 For the last time, villain, avoid my sight,
Leave me; or force a father in his rage
To have you flung with infamy from the place.
Exit HIPPOLYTUS

THESEUS *alone*

And now you go towards your waiting doom
Irrevocably. For by that River's name
Terrible even to the immortal Gods,

1160 Un Dieu vengeur te suit, tu ne peux l'éviter.
Je t'aimais. Et je sens que malgré ton offense
Mes entrailles pour toi se troublent par avance.
Mais à te condamner tu m'as trop engagé.
Jamais père en effet fut-il plus outragé ?
Justes Dieux, qui voyez la douleur qui m'accable,
Ai-je pu mettre au jour un enfant si coupable ?

SCÈNE IV
PHÈDRE, THÉSÉE

PHÈDRE
Seigneur, je viens à vous pleine d'un juste effroi.
Votre voix redoutable a passé jusqu'à moi.
Je crains qu'un prompt effet n'ait suivi la menace.
1170 S'il en est temps encore, épargnez votre race.
Respectez votre sang, j'ose vous en prier.
Sauvez-moi de l'horreur de l'entendre crier.
Ne me préparez point la douleur éternelle
De l'avoir fait répandre à la main paternelle.
THÉSÉE
Non, Madame, en mon sang ma main n'a point trempé.
Mais l'ingrat toutefois ne m'est point échappé.
Une immortelle main de sa perte est chargée.
Neptune me la doit, et vous serez vengée.
PHÈDRE
Neptune vous la doit ! Quoi ! vos vœux irrités . . .
THÉSÉE
1180 Quoi ! craignez-vous déjà qu'ils ne soient écoutés ?
Joignez-vous bien plutôt à mes vœux légitimes.
Dans toute leur noirceur retracez-moi ses crimes.
Échauffez mes transports trop lents, trop retenus.
Tous ses crimes encor ne vous sont pas connus.
Sa fureur contre vous se répand en injures.
Votre bouche, dit-il, est pleine d'impostures.
Il soutient qu'Aricie a son cœur, a sa foi,
Qu'il l'aime.
PHÈDRE
                    Quoi, Seigneur !
THÉSÉE
                                        Il l'a dit devant moi.

Neptune has sworn his oath, and will perform it.
Yes, and I loved you, and in spite of all,
Before the hour is come, my bowels yearn
For pity of you. But I have too much cause—
1180 Did ever a deeper injury wound a father?
Ye righteous Gods, that see me thus prostrated,
Did I give being to a son like this?

Enter PHAEDRA

PHAEDRA
My lord, you see me here impelled by terror:
Just now, when that terrible voice assailed my ears,
I thought the threat might come to a fulfilment.
Let me beg you, if there still is time, have pity
On your own race, save your own flesh; spare me,
My lord, the dreadful cry of murdered blood,
Spare me the endless misery of laying
1190 That horrible stain on a paternal hand.
THESEUS
My lady, I have kept my hand unstained
And still the unnatural boy has not escaped;
Immortal hands will undertake his doom,
Neptune's my debtor; you shall be avenged.
PHAEDRA
Your debtor, Neptune! Then your prayer of hate . . .
THESEUS
Are you afraid it might be heard too soon?
No, join your own entreaty with my curses,
Paint me his crimes once more in all their blackness
Inflame my faint and still-too-sluggish rage—
1200 He has added guilt more than the guilt you knew:
His frenzy spends itself in railing on you,
He swears that all your words are perjuries,
He says Aricia claims his heart, his love,
His loyalty.
PHAEDRA
            No, my lord!
THESEUS
                        That is what he told me;

Mais je sais rejeter un frivole artifice.
1190 Espérons de Neptune une prompte justice.
Je vais moi-même encore au pied de ses autels
Le presser d'accomplir ses serments immortels.

SCÈNE V
PHÈDRE *seule*

Il sort. Quelle nouvelle a frappé mon oreille ?
Quel feu mal étouffé dans mon cœur se réveille ?
Quel coup de foudre, ô Ciel ! et quel funeste avis !
Je volais toute entière au secours de son fils.
Et m'arrachant des bras d'Œnone épouvantée
Je cédais au remords dont j'étais tourmentée.
Qui sait même où m'allait porter ce repentir ?
1200 Peut-être à m'accuser j'aurais pu consentir,
Peut-être si la voix ne m'eût été coupée,
L'affreuse vérité me serait échappée.
Hippolyte est sensible, et ne sent rien pour moi !
Aricie a son cœur ! Aricie a sa foi !
Ah Dieux ! Lorsqu'à mes vœux l'ingrat inexorable
S'armait d'un œil si fier, d'un front si redoutable,
Je pensais qu'à l'amour son cœur toujours fermé,
Fût contre tout mon sexe également armé.
Une autre cependant a fléchi son audace.
1210 Devant ses yeux cruels une autre a trouvé grâce.
Peut-être a-t-il un cœur facile à s'attendrir.
Je suis le seul objet qu'il ne saurait souffrir.
Et je me chargerais du soin de le défendre !

SCÈNE VI
PHÈDRE, ŒNONE

PHÈDRE
Chère Œnone, sais-tu ce que je viens d'apprendre ?
ŒNONE
Non. Mais je viens tremblante, à ne vous point mentir.
J'ai pâli du dessein qui vous a fait sortir.
J'ai craint une fureur à vous-même fatale.
PHÈDRE
Œnone, qui l'eût cru ? J'avais une rivale.

Not that a flimsy lie could impose on me.
I hope to hear that Neptune's justice falls
Swiftly, and till that hour I'll ply his altars
And keep him mindful of his undying word.
Exit

PHAEDRA *alone*

He leaves me, with this dreadful news, alone.
1210 Ah Gods, the fire that I dreamed was safely stifled
To wake no more! Dreadful, unlooked-for news!
All trepidation and remorse, all speed
Out of Oenone's clinging arms of fear
I came to save his son. And who can tell
What might have been had conscience had its way?
Whether I might have spoken of my guilt,
Might have let slip, had he but left me time,
The entire and awful truth?—He has felt love,
Hippolytus, who never felt for me;
1220 Aricia claims his loyalty, his love . . .
Gods! while I pleaded, while my prayer beat
On those rigid eyes, that unrelenting brow,
I thought he bore impenetrable armour
Always the same and closed to all alike.
And now another has overthrown his pride,
Another finds favour in the tyrant's eyes;
Perhaps his heart is easy to entreat
And condescends to any plea but mine.
And I am fool enough to be his friend!
1230 —Oenone, do you know what I have heard?

Enter OENONE

OENONE
No; I have tried to find you in alarm,
Wondering what sudden impulse drove you here
And how it may imperil you . . .
    PHAEDRA
                        Oenone,
Who would have thought there was another woman?

ŒNONE

Comment ?

PHÈDRE

    Hippolyte aime, et je n'en puis douter.
1220 Ce farouche ennemi qu'on ne pouvait dompter,
Qu'offensait le respect, qu'importunait la plainte,
Ce tigre, que jamais je n'abordai sans crainte,
Soumis, apprivoisé reconnaît un vainqueur.
Aricie a trouvé le chemin de son cœur.

ŒNONE

Aricie ?

PHÈDRE

    Ah, douleur non encore éprouvée !
A quel nouveau tourment je me suis réservée !
Tout ce que j'ai souffert, mes craintes, mes transports,
La fureur de mes feux, l'horreur de mes remords,
Et d'un refus cruel l'insupportable injure
1230 N'était qu'un faible essai du tourment que j'endure.
Ils s'aiment ! Par quel charme ont-ils trompé mes yeux ?
Comment se sont-ils vus ? Depuis quand ? Dans quels lieux ?
Tu le savais. Pourquoi me laissais-tu séduire ?
De leur furtive ardeur ne pouvais-tu m'instruire ?
Les a-t-on vu souvent se parler, se chercher ?
Dans le fond des forêts allaient-ils se cacher ?
Hélas ! Ils se voyaient avec pleine licence.
Le ciel de leurs soupirs approuvait l'innocence.
Ils suivaient sans remords leur penchant amoureux.
1240 Tous les jours se levaient clairs et sereins pour eux.
Et moi, triste rebut de la Nature entière,
Je me cachais au jour, je fuyais la lumière.
La Mort est le seul Dieu que j'osais implorer.
J'attendais le moment où j'allais expirer.
Me nourrissant de fiel, de larmes abreuvée,
Encor dans mon malheur de trop près observée,
Je n'osais dans mes pleurs me noyer à loisir,
Je goûtais en tremblant ce funeste plaisir.
Et sous un front serein déguisant mes alarmes,
1250 Il fallait bien souvent me priver de mes larmes.

ŒNONE

Quel fruit recevront-ils de leurs vaines amours ?
Ils ne se verront plus.

OENONE

You say—

PHAEDRA

       Hippolytus, I tell you, loves—
The adversary I could never shake,
Vexed by submission, impatient of complaining,
The ogre that I never could encounter
1240 Undaunted; he is tamed and brought to heel,
Aricia has forced the access to his heart.

OENONE

Aricia!

PHAEDRA

       Oh, I never thought of these,
These newest tortures that I live to taste:
All the old despairs, the ecstasies, the broodings,
Raging of flame, and horror of remorse,
And that slight of unendurable denial
Were barely foretastes of my torment here.
They, lovers! Did they bewitch these watchful eyes?
What time did they find to meet? Since when? What place?
What furtive means? You knew. Why was I left
1250 To treasure foolish dreams? You might have told me
Of their stolen pleasure. Were they often seen
Speaking, or lingering? Was it the forest shades
That sheltered them? Ah, but they had liberty
To see the face they sought. The Heavens smiled
On the innocence of their embrace, no fear
Restrained their eager steps, and each fair day
Rose clear and candid on their love. And I
Disowned, dishonoured in the whole creation
I fled the sun, I could not face the daylight,
1260 Death was the only godhead I could pray;
Gall on my tongue, and tears my only drink;
Happy, if any privacy of grief
Had left me this one pitiable solace,
To taste a last precarious luxury;
But the forced travesty of a smiling face
Deprived me even of the right to weep.

OENONE

They reap no harvest of their vain desires:
They'll meet no more.

PHÈDRE

                Ils s'aimeront toujours.
Au moment que je parle, ah, mortelle pensée!
Ils bravent la fureur d'une amante insensée.
Malgré ce même exil qui va les écarter,
Ils font mille serments de ne se point quitter.
Non, je ne puis souffrir un bonheur qui m'outrage,
Œnone. Prends pitié de ma jalouse rage.
Il faut perdre Aricie. Il faut de mon époux
1260 Contre un sang odieux réveiller le courroux.
Qu'il ne se borne pas à des peines légères.
Le crime de la sœur passe celui des frères.
Dans mes jaloux transports je le veux implorer.
    Que fais-je? Où ma raison se va-t-elle égarer?
Moi jalouse! Et Thésée est celui que j'implore!
Mon époux est vivant, et moi je brûle encore!
Pour qui? Quel est le cœur où prétendent mes vœux?
Chaque mot sur mon front fait dresser mes cheveux.
Mes crimes désormais ont comblé la mesure.
1270 Je respire à la fois l'inceste et l'imposture.
Mes homicides mains promptes à me venger
Dans le sang innocent brûlent de se plonger.
Misérable! Et je vis? Et je soutiens la vue
De ce sacré Soleil dont je suis descendue?
J'ai pour aïeul le Père et le Maître des Dieux.
Le Ciel, tout l'Univers est plein de mes aïeux.
Où me cacher? Fuyons dans la nuit infernale.
Mais que dis-je? Mon père y tient l'urne fatale.
Le sort, dit-on, l'a mise en ses sévères mains.
1280 Minos juge aux Enfers tous les pâles humains.
Ah! combien frémira son ombre épouvantée,
Lorsqu'il verra sa fille à ses yeux présentée,
Contrainte d'avouer tant de forfaits divers,
Et des crimes peut-être inconnus aux Enfers?
Que diras-tu, mon père, à ce spectacle horrible?
Je crois voir de ta main tomber l'urne terrible,
Je crois te voir cherchant un supplice nouveau,
Toi-même de ton sang devenir le bourreau.
Pardonne. Un Dieu cruel a perdu ta famille.
1290 Reconnais sa vengeance aux fureurs de ta fille.
Hélas! Du crime affreux dont la honte me suit,

PHAEDRA

               They'll love for evermore.
Now as I speak—the poison of the thought!—
1270 Mocking the fury of a rival wronged,
Forgetful of the exile that divides them,
They swear a thousand times never to part.
No, I will not yield to the insult of their joy,
Oenone. Help me, pity my jealousy.
Aricia must be crushed. I must stir up
My husband's wrath against that hated house—
No feeble sentence serves, the sister's crime
Is more than all her brothers'. I'll entreat him
In rage and jealousy.
               What am I doing?
1280 Where is reason in my wandering mind? I, jealous?
I, entreat Theseus? He, my husband, lives
And still I love—and whom? Still yearn—for whom?
At every word each separate hair lifts up
Upon my head. My guilt has filled the measure—
I crave for incest, dream of calumny,
My murderous hands, avid for vengeance, burn
To bathe in the blood of innocence. Misery!
And dare I live, and dare I face the sight
Of that sacred Sun, the giver of my life,
1290 I, grandchild of the high Father of the Gods,
My forbears crowding Heaven and all creation?
Where may I hide? Flee to the night of Hell?
No, no, not there; for there my father's hands
Inexorable lift the doomsday urn,
They say, and Minos stands in deathly justice
Over the pallid multitudes of men.
Will that great shade not start in ghastly anger
When I in shame before his awful gaze,
His daughter, plead my guilt, and deeds perhaps
1300 Unheard in all the calendar of Hell?
Father, what will you say to these? I see
The tremendous urn roll thundering at your feet;
I see you ponder unknown penalties
To execute yourself upon your own . . .
Forgive. A cruel God detests your seed,
A heavenly vengeance breathed in me the frenzy

Jamais mon triste cœur n'a recueilli le fruit.
Jusqu'au dernier soupir de malheurs poursuivie,
Je rends dans les tourments une pénible vie.

ŒNONE

Hé! repoussez, Madame, une injuste terreur.
Regardez d'un autre œil une excusable erreur.
Vous aimez. On ne peut vaincre sa destinée.
Par un charme fatal vous fûtes entraînée.
Est-ce donc un prodige inouï parmi nous?
1300 L'amour n'a-t-il encor triomphé que de vous?
La faiblesse aux humains n'est que trop naturelle.
Mortelle, subissez le sort d'une mortelle.
Vous vous plaignez d'un joug imposé dès longtemps.
Les Dieux même, les Dieux de l'Olympe habitants,
Qui d'un bruit si terrible épouvantent les crimes,
Ont brûlé quelquefois de feux illégitimes.

PHÈDRE

Qu'entends-je? Quels conseils ose-t-on me donner?
Ainsi donc jusqu'au bout tu veux m'empoisonner,
Malheureuse? Voilà comme tu m'as perdue.
1310 Au jour que je fuyais c'est toi qui m'as rendue.
Tes prières m'ont fait oublier mon devoir.
J'évitais Hippolyte, et tu me l'as fait voir.
De quoi te chargeais-tu? Pourquoi ta bouche impie
A-t-elle en l'accusant osé noircir sa vie?
Il en mourra peut-être, et d'un père insensé
Le sacrilège vœu peut-être est exaucé.
Je ne t'écoute plus. Va-t'en, Monstre exécrable.
Va, laisse-moi le soin de mon sort déplorable.
Puisse le juste Ciel dignement te payer;
1320 Et puisse ton supplice à jamais effrayer
Tous ceux qui, comme toi, par de lâches adresses,
Des Princes malheureux nourrissent les faiblesses,
Les poussent au penchant où leur cœur est enclin,
Et leur osent du crime aplanir le chemin;
Détestables flatteurs, présent le plus funeste
Que puisse faire aux Rois la colère céleste.

ŒNONE *seule*

Ah, Dieux! Pour la servir j'ai tout fait, tout quitté.
Et j'en reçois ce prix? Je l'ai bien mérité.

Fin du quatrième Acte

You see. Alas, and still of all the guilt
And all the shame that never will release me
My fearful heart has never reaped the sweets.
1310 Pursued while yet I breathe by ceaseless evils
I wait to yield a bruised and broken life.

OENONE

My lady, come, dismiss a causeless terror,
Be more indulgent to a venial failing—
You love; but driven by a fatal charm.
It is not ours to challenge Destiny.
Was this a wonder never seen till now?
Were you the first that Love has overthrown?
Weakness was always part of man's inheritance;
So, mortal, bow to a mortal's destiny.
1320 You struggle against an immemorial yoke:
Even the Gods that live in high Olympus
Whose judgements hold a guilty world in fear
Have loved, and sometimes loved against the law.

PHAEDRA

Still you dare speak? And this is your advice,
And till the end you mean to drug my mind?
I hate you. All your help has been my downfall.
You dragged me back to the unbearable sunshine;
Your prayers were louder than the voice of right;
The man that I had shunned, you made me see.
1330 Was it your business? And now have all the lies
Of those false lips dared blacken such a life?
You may have killed him. His father's impious vows
And blind revenge perhaps are gratified
Already. I'll hear no more. Leave me alone,
Loathly inhuman temptress; leave my sight,
Leave me alone to shape my bitter future.
On you I pray the justice of the Gods;
And may they make you the eternal warning
Of all cringing cunning sycophants that nourish
1340 Their masters' dearest weakness, urge the way
Their cravings tend, and smooth the slope of crime,
Accursed courtiers, deadliest gift of all
That angry Heaven inflicts upon a King! *Exit*

OENONE

O ye Gods! To have borne so much for her, forgone
So much!—This is my pay. And it is just.

SCÈNE PREMIÈRE
HIPPOLYTE, ARICIE

ARICIE

Quoi! vous pouvez vous taire en ce péril extrême?
1330 Vous laissez dans l'erreur un père qui vous aime?
Cruel, si de mes pleurs méprisant le pouvoir
Vous consentez sans peine à ne me plus revoir,
Partez, séparez-vous de la triste Aricie.
Mais du moins en partant assurez votre vie.
Défendez votre honneur d'un reproche honteux,
Et forcez votre père à révoquer ses vœux.
Il en est temps encor. Pourquoi? Par quel caprice
Laissez-vous le champ libre à votre accusatrice?
Éclaircissez Thésée.

HIPPOLYTE

                                    Hé! que n'ai-je point dit?
1340 Ai-je dû mettre au jour l'opprobre de son lit?
Devais-je, en lui faisant un récit trop sincère,
D'une indigne rougeur couvrir le front d'un père?
Vous seule avez percé ce mystère odieux.
Mon cœur pour s'épancher n'a que vous et les Dieux.
Je n'ai pu vous cacher, jugez si je vous aime,
Tout ce que je voulais me cacher à moi-même.
Mais songez sous quel sceau je vous l'ai révélé.
Oubliez, s'il se peut, que je vous ai parlé,
Madame. Et que jamais une bouche si pure
1350 Ne s'ouvre pour conter cette horrible aventure.
Sur l'équité des Dieux osons nous confier.
Ils ont trop d'intérêt à me justifier;
Et Phèdre tôt ou tard de son crime punie,

Act Five

ARICIA
And in this extremity you will not speak
And will not undeceive a loving father?
Cruel, if you can disregard my tears
And lightly say good-bye to me for ever,
1350 Then go, and leave Aricia with her grief;
But do not go in certainty of death.
Fight the foul imputation on your honour,
Constrain your father to unsay his curses.
There is time yet. What reason, or what folly
Makes you leave all the advantage to the accuser?
Tell Theseus what you know.

HIPPOLYTUS
                 Have I not told
What may be told? Would you have me reveal
To light the shameful mystery of his bed
Or by too scrupulous report bring down
1360 Confusion on a father's honoured head?
Alone you know this horror. You, and the Gods,
Alone receive the outpourings of my heart.
See if I love you: I have shown to you
What I would fain have veiled from my own thoughts.
But under what a seal, you know. Forget,
My lady, if you can, that I have spoken;
Let me believe this hideous affair
Will never be breathed between those blameless lips.
We set our trust upon the righteous heavens.
1370 My cause is theirs; and Phaedra, whether soon
Or in the slow procedure of their justice,

N'en saurait éviter la juste ignominie.
C'est l'unique respect que j'exige de vous.
Je permets tout le reste à mon libre courroux.
Sortez de l'esclavage où vous êtes réduite.
Osez me suivre. Osez accompagner ma fuite.
Arrachez-vous d'un lieu funeste et profané,
1360 Où la Vertu respire un air empoisonné.
Profitez pour cacher votre prompte retraite,
De la confusion que ma disgrâce y jette.
Je vous puis de la fuite assurer les moyens,
Vous n'avez jusqu'ici de gardes que les miens.
De puissants défenseurs prendront notre querelle.
Argos nous tend les bras, et Sparte nous appelle.
A nos amis communs portons nos justes cris.
Ne souffrons pas que Phèdre assemblant nos débris
Du trône paternel nous chasse l'un et l'autre,
1370 Et promette à son fils ma dépouille et la vôtre.
L'occasion est belle, il la faut embrasser.
Quelle peur vous retient ? Vous semblez balancer ?
Votre seul intérêt m'inspire cette audace.
Quand je suis tout de feu, d'où vous vient cette glace ?
Sur les pas d'un banni craignez-vous de marcher ?

ARICIE

Hélas ! qu'un tel exil, Seigneur, me serait cher !
Dans quels ravissements, à votre sort liée
Du reste des mortels je vivrais oubliée !
Mais n'étant point unis par un lien si doux,
1380 Me puis-je avec honneur dérober avec vous ?
Je sais que sans blesser l'honneur le plus sévère
Je me puis affranchir des mains de votre père.
Ce n'est point m'arracher du sein de mes parents,
Et la fuite est permise à qui fuit ses Tyrans ;
Mais vous m'aimez, Seigneur. Et ma gloire alarmée . . .

HIPPOLYTE

Non, non ; j'ai trop de soin de votre renommée.
Un plus noble dessein m'amène devant vous.
Fuyez vos ennemis, et suivez votre époux.
Libres dans nos malheurs, puisque le ciel l'ordonne,
1390 Le don de notre foi ne dépend de personne.
L'Hymen n'est point toujours entouré de flambeaux.
   Aux portes de Trézène, et parmi ces tombeaux,

Will not elude disgrace. This deference
I ask of you; and all the rest I sweep
Before the liberty of my wrath. I bid you
No longer be a slave. I bid you dare
To come with me, dare to be banned with me.
Break from a poisoned house where Virtue breathes
A deathly and a desecrated air;
Turn into profit for a headlong flight
1380 All the disorder following on my fall.
The means I offer: you have still no guard
But my own men. Most powerful patrons wait us—
Argos extends her arms, and Sparta welcomes;
Let common friends receive our just laments,
Otherwise Phaedra rakes our wreckage up,
Evicts us both from a throne our fathers left us,
And strips us both for spoils to deck her son.
The moment beckons, grasp it. But what fear
Restrains you? What suspends your doubtful mind?
1390 Only for your sake have I dared so far.
When I am all on fire, why are you ice?
Are you unwilling to adventure on
An outlaw's path?

ARICIA

           Oh, but how happily,
My lord, I'd taste of exile so; how eagerly
Embrace a life forgotten of all beside
And linked with yours! But lacking that sweet bond
Can I in honour join your wanderings?
I know the sternest laws do not forbid me
To fly your father's power: he is not mine,
1400 I owe him no obedience; and to fly
From an oppressor is the right of all.
But you, my lord, love me. And anxious honour . . .

HIPPOLYTUS

And can you think I rate that honour cheaply?
No, no. I came with worthier designs—
Escape your foes, and follow as my bride.
Free in adversity, since Fate has freed us,
Our pledges need no words but ours, and Hymen
Robbed of his torchlit rites is Hymen still.
By Trozen's gates, among those sepulchres,

Des Princes de ma race antiques sépultures,
Est un temple sacré formidable aux parjures.
C'est là que les mortels n'osent jurer en vain.
Le perfide y reçoit un châtiment soudain.
Et craignant d'y trouver la mort inévitable,
Le mensonge n'a point de frein plus redoutable.
Là, si vous m'en croyez, d'un amour éternel
1400 Nous irons confirmer le serment solennel.
Nous prendrons à témoin le Dieu qu'on y révère.
Nous le prierons tous deux de nous servir de père.
Des Dieux les plus sacrés j'attesterai le nom.
Et la chaste Diane, et l'auguste Junon,
Et tous les Dieux enfin témoins de mes tendresses
Garantiront la foi de mes saintes promesses.

ARICIE

Le Roi vient. Fuyez, Prince, et partez promptement.
Pour cacher mon départ je demeure un moment.
Allez, et laissez-moi quelque fidèle guide,
1410 Qui conduise vers vous ma démarche timide.

SCÈNE II
THÉSÉE, ARICIE, ISMÈNE

THÉSÉE

Dieux, éclairez mon trouble, et daignez à mes yeux
Montrer la vérité, que je cherche en ces lieux.

ARICIE

Songe à tout, chère Ismène, et sois prête à la fuite.

SCÈNE III
THÉSÉE, ARICIE

THÉSÉE

Vous changez de couleur, et semblez interdite,
Madame! Que faisait Hippolyte en ce lieu?

ARICIE

Seigneur, il me disait un éternel adieu.

THÉSÉE

Vos yeux ont su dompter ce rebelle courage;
Et ses premiers soupirs sont votre heureux ouvrage.

ARICIE

Seigneur, je ne vous puis nier la vérité.

1410 Antique memorials of my fathers' pride,
A wayside temple holy and renowned
Stands grim protector of the plighted word;
There falsehood dare not raise her voice, or falls
Blasted at once, and certitude of death
Lays chains invincible on perjury.
May we not there with solemn mutual oath
Give and receive our hearts' enduring faith
Before the shrine, and pray the Deity
For his protection and paternal love?

1420 I will invoke each mighty God to hear me—
Maiden Diana, Juno's majesty,
And every name whose present patronage
Shall seal and sanctify my true intent.

ARICIA

The King is here. Go, Prince, depart at once.
I shall remain awhile to hide my purpose.
Away—but send me back a trusty servant
To guide my footsteps safely to your side.

Exit HIPPOLYTUS

Enter THESEUS

THESEUS

Lighten the mists, ye Gods, and show my eyes
The truth they seek for here!

ARICIA

                              Now, sweet Ismene,
1430 See everything is done. Be ready quickly.

Exit ISMENE

THESEUS

You seem disturbed, your colour fails, my lady.
What was Hippolytus doing in this place?

ARICIA

Taking an everlasting leave, my lord.

THESEUS

And so your eyes have tamed that rebel heart
And brought him to his earliest thoughts of love.

ARICIA

I must not hide the truth from you, my lord.

1420 De votre injuste haine il n'a pas hérité.
Il ne me traitait point comme une criminelle.

THÉSÉE

J'entends, il vous jurait une amour éternelle.
Ne vous assurez point sur ce cœur inconstant.
Car à d'autres que vous il en jurait autant.

ARICIE

Lui, Seigneur ?

THÉSÉE

             Vous deviez le rendre moins volage.
Comment souffriez-vous cet horrible partage ?

ARICIE

Et comment souffrez-vous que d'horribles discours
D'une si belle vie osent noircir le cours ?
Avez-vous de son cœur si peu de connaissance ?
1430 Discernez-vous si mal le crime et l'innocence ?
Faut-il qu'à vos yeux seuls un nuage odieux
Dérobe sa vertu qui brille à tous les yeux ?
Ah ! c'est trop le livrer à des langues perfides.
Cessez. Repentez-vous de vos vœux homicides.
Craignez, Seigneur, craignez que le Ciel rigoureux
Ne vous haïsse assez pour exaucer vos vœux.
Souvent dans sa colère il reçoit nos victimes.
Ses présents sont souvent la peine de nos crimes.

THÉSÉE

Non, vous voulez en vain couvrir son attentat.
1440 Votre amour vous aveugle en faveur de l'ingrat.
Mais j'en crois des témoins certains, irréprochables.
J'ai vu, j'ai vu couler des larmes véritables.

ARICIE

Prenez garde, Seigneur. Vos invincibles mains
Ont de Monstres sans nombre affranchi les humains.
Mais tout n'est pas détruit; Et vous en laissez vivre
Un . . . Votre fils, Seigneur, me défend de poursuivre.
Instruite du respect qu'il veut vous conserver,
Je l'affligerais trop, si j'osais achever.
J'imite sa pudeur, et fuis votre présence
1450 Pour n'être pas forcée à rompre le silence.

You have not given him your unjust hatred;
He did not treat me like a criminal.

THESEUS

You mean he vowed you everlasting passion.
1440 I should not build on that unsettled heart.
He swore as deep to others.

ARICIA

He, my lord?

THESEUS

I wish you could have taught him constancy.
How could you bear that loathsome competition?

ARICIA

And how can you bear loathsome calumnies
To blacken all the lustre of his fame?
Have you so little knowledge of his nature?
Can you not tell the guiltless from the guilty?
Only your eyes are darkened by a cloud
That lets his goodness gleam on all the world.
1450 Oh stop, relent. He must not be the victim
Of false accusers. Repent your murderous curses.
Tremble, my lord, tremble, lest frowning Heaven
Hate you enough to take you at your word—
Gods may accept our offerings in anger
And punish with the presents we entreated.

THESEUS

No, blind as you are with ill-requited love
You will not blind me to his villainy;
For I have witnesses, beyond reproach,
Beyond suspicion—I have seen tears flow,
1460 Tears that were true.

ARICIA

Look to yourself, my lord:
Your matchless weight of arm redeemed mankind
From monsters past all counting—but not all,
The breed is not destroyed, and you have saved
One. . . . I must say no more; your son forbids me.
Knowing what deference his heart still holds
I should increase his suffering too much
Dared I continue. Let me imitate
His generous scruple, and excuse myself
While nothing forces me to break my silence.   *Exit*

SCÈNE IV

THÉSÉE *seul*

Quelle est donc sa pensée ? Et que cache un discours
Commencé tant de fois, interrompu toujours ?
Veulent-ils m'éblouir par une feinte vaine ?
Sont-ils d'accord tous deux pour me mettre à la gêne ?
Mais moi-même, malgré ma sévère rigueur,
Quelle plaintive voix crie au fond de mon cœur ?
Une pitié secrète et m'afflige, et m'étonne.
Une seconde fois interrogeons Œnone.
Je veux de tout le crime être mieux éclairci.
1460 Gardes. Qu'Œnone sorte et vienne seule ici.

SCÈNE V

THÉSÉE, PANOPE

PANOPE

J'ignore le projet que la Reine médite,
Seigneur. Mais je crains tout du transport qui l'agite.
Un mortel désespoir sur son visage est peint.
La pâleur de la mort est déjà sur son teint.
Déjà de sa présence avec honte chassée
Dans la profonde mer Œnone s'est lancée.
On ne sait point d'où part ce dessein furieux.
Et les flots pour jamais l'ont ravie à nos yeux.

THÉSÉE

Qu'entends-je ?

PANOPE

Son trépas n'a point calmé la Reine.
1470 Le trouble semble croître en son âme incertaine.
Quelquefois pour flatter ses secrètes douleurs
Elle prend ses enfants, et les baigne de pleurs.
Et soudain renonçant à l'amour maternelle,
Sa main avec horreur les repousse loin d'elle.
Elle porte au hasard ses pas irrésolus.
Son œil tout égaré ne nous reconnaît plus.
Elle a trois fois écrit, et changeant de pensée
Trois fois elle a rompu sa lettre commencée.
Daignez la voir, Seigneur, daignez la secourir.

THESEUS *alone*

1470 But what is in her mind? What lurks below
A tale so often broached, and never told?
Is it a stratagem without a meaning?
Is it conspiracy to bind me on
A rack of doubt? And secret in my heart
Steeled to be cruel, what is the still voice
That pleads for mercy, and unmans my wrath,
Perplexes me and tears me?—I must see
Her woman once again; I know too little.
—Guard! Fetch Oenone, send her in alone.

Enter PANOPE

PANOPE

1480 I cannot say what thoughts are in her bosom,
But the distracted motions of the Queen
Fill me with fear, my lord. Death and despair
Are painted on her face, and the deathly tint
Sits even now upon her cheeks. Already
Pursued with scorn and chiding from her side,
Oenone has plunged to death among the waves.
None knows what wild will drove her, but the tide
Has covered her for ever from our sight.

THESEUS

What have you said?

PANOPE

Her going gave no peace;

1490 Distraction gains in the Queen's divided soul:
One moment, soothing her mysterious grief,
She takes her children, bathes them in her tears;
And suddenly, her motherhood dismissed,
She drives them from her with a look of loathing.
Her restless steps come and go purposeless
And we are strangers in her fevered eyes.
Thrice she has written, only to repent,
And thrice destroyed the message uncompleted.
My lord, be gracious: see her, comfort her.

THÉSÉE

1480 O Ciel! Œnone est morte, et Phèdre veut mourir ?
Qu'on rappelle mon fils, qu'il vienne se défendre,
Qu'il vienne me parler, je suis prêt de l'entendre.
Ne précipite point tes funestes bienfaits,
Neptune. J'aime mieux n'être exaucé jamais.
J'ai peut-être trop cru des témoins peu fidèles.
Et j'ai trop tôt vers toi levé mes mains cruelles.
Ah! de quel désespoir mes vœux seraient suivis !

SCÈNE VI
THÉSÉE, THÉRAMÈNE

THÉSÉE

Théramène est-ce toi ? Qu'as-tu fait de mon fils ?
Je te l'ai confié dès l'âge le plus tendre.
1490 Mais d'où naissent les pleurs que je te vois répandre ?
Que fait mon fils ?

THÉRAMÈNE

O soins tardifs, et superflus !
Inutile tendresse ! Hippolyte n'est plus.

THÉSÉE

Dieux !

THÉRAMÈNE

J'ai vu des mortels périr le plus aimable,
Et j'ose dire encor, Seigneur, le moins coupable.

THÉSÉE

Mon fils n'est plus ? Hé quoi! quand je lui tends les bras,
Les Dieux impatients ont hâté son trépas ?
Quel coup me l'a ravi ? Quelle foudre soudaine ?

THÉRAMÈNE

A peine nous sortions des portes de Trézène,
Il était sur son char. Ses gardes affligés
1500 Imitaient son silence, autour de lui rangés.
Il suivait tout pensif le chemin de Mycènes.
Sa main sur ses chevaux laissait flotter les rênes.
Ses superbes coursiers, qu'on voyait autrefois
Pleins d'une ardeur si noble obéir à sa voix,

THESEUS

1500 Is it so? The one is dead, the other waits
For death. Call for my son, let him plead his cause,
Let him speak to me, and I will listen.—Neptune,
Delay thy deadly gift, be not too sudden,
Rather refuse it utterly. What if
I was seduced too soon by worthless words?
What if my cruel hands were raised too rashly?
What wretchedness would follow from that vow!

Enter THERAMENES. *Exit* PANOPE

THESEUS

Is it you, Theramenes? Where is my son?
What have you done with him? His careful tending
1510 Has been your charge from earliest infancy.
But why the tears I see upon your cheeks?
What of my son?

THERAMENES

O late, O vain regret,
O useless love! The Prince's life is done.

THESEUS

Oh Gods!

THERAMENES

I saw him die, the best and sweetest
Of human kind—and, let me say, my lord,
The purest also.

THESEUS

Is my son dead? Now,
Now that these arms reached out for him, the Gods
Impatient urged his execution on?
How did I lose him? What immortal stroke . . .?

THERAMENES

1520 Still close behind us lay the gates of Trozen.
He drove his chariot, his grieving guard
Matching his silence, marched on either hand.
Sunk in his thought, the loose reins lying free,
He brought us on the causeway to Mycenae;
And the noble beasts, so eager once to leap
At the least inflexion of a master's voice,

L'œil morne maintenant et la tête baissée
Semblaient se conformer à sa triste pensée.
Un effroyable cri sorti du fond des flots
Des airs en ce moment a troublé le repos ;
Et du sein de la terre une voix formidable
1510 Répond en gémissant à ce cri redoutable.
Jusqu'au fond de nos cœurs notre sang s'est glacé.
Des coursiers attentifs le crin s'est hérissé.
Cependant sur le dos de la plaine liquide
S'élève à gros bouillons une montagne humide.
L'onde approche, se brise, et vomit à nos yeux
Parmi des flots d'écume un Monstre furieux.
Son front large est armé de cornes menaçantes.
Tout son corps est couvert d'écailles jaunissantes.
Indomptable Taureau, Dragon impétueux,
1520 Sa croupe se recourbe en replis tortueux.
Ses longs mugissements font trembler le rivage.
Le ciel avec horreur voit ce Monstre sauvage,
La terre s'en émeut, l'air en est infecté,
Le flot, qui l'apporta, recule épouvanté.
Tout fuit, et sans s'armer d'un courage inutile
Dans le temple voisin chacun cherche un asile.
Hippolyte lui seul digne fils d'un héros,
Arrête ses coursiers, saisit ses javelots,
Pousse au Monstre, et d'un dard lancé d'une main sûre
1530 Il lui fait dans le flanc une large blessure.
De rage et de douleur le Monstre bondissant
Vient aux pieds des chevaux tomber en mugissant,
Se roule, et leur présente une gueule enflammée,
Qui les couvre de feu, de sang, et de fumée.
La frayeur les emporte, et sourds à cette fois,
Ils ne connaissent plus ni le frein ni la voix.
En efforts impuissants leur maître se consume.
Ils rougissent le mors d'une sanglante écume.
On dit qu'on a vu même en ce désordre affreux
1540 Un Dieu, qui d'aiguillons pressait leur flanc poudreux.
A travers des rochers la peur les précipite.
L'essieu crie, et se rompt. L'intrépide Hippolyte
Voit voler en éclats tout son char fracassé.
Dans les rênes lui-même il tombe embarrassé.
Excusez ma douleur. Cette image cruelle

Now bent dull eyes to earth and drooping crests
As if communing with his bitter mood.
—Suddenly from the sea an awful cry
1530 Shattered the silence of the air. And then
A second voice wailed answer from the landward.
Our blood was frozen in our inmost hearts.
Stiffly uprose the listening horses' manes.
And now from the level deep immense there heaves
A boiling mount of brine, and still it swells,
Bears wavelike foaming down on us and breaks
To belch a ravening monster at our feet
Whose threatening brow is broadened with huge horns,
Whose body, cased in golden glint of scales,
1540 Thrashes a train of sinuous writhing whorls.
Indomitable bull, malignant dragon,
Its long-drawn bellows rumble down the shore;
Heaven quails, earth shudders at the portent, air
Reeks with its pestilential breath. The wave
Withdraws again, aghast at what it bore.
We fly to the nearby temple; not one lingers
Or wraps himself in unavailing valour.
Hippolytus, honouring his hero blood,
Hippolytus alone checks, wheels his team,
1550 Snatches the spears, charges upon the creature,
Aims, and unerring flings. A gaping slash
Fair in the monster's flank drives it in bounds
Of pain and fury to the horses' feet
To roar and wallow and gnash with flaming jaws
And spatter them with blood and cloud and fire.
They plunge reckless aside. They hear no more,
Answer no more to bridle or to voice.
The charioteer spends all his strength in strivings
While they redden the bits with spume that is bright with blood.
1560 Even, men say, some more than mortal shape
Borne on the horrible confusion plied
Their dusty flanks with goads. Where terror leads them
Stand rocks. The axle screeches, snaps. The car
Crashes in fragments; and my fearless master
Drops tangled in the reins . . .—Forgive my weakness.
In that tormenting image lives a source

Sera pour moi de pleurs une source éternelle.
J'ai vu, Seigneur, j'ai vu votre malheureux fils
Traîné par les chevaux que sa main a nourris.
Il veut les rappeler, et sa voix les effraie.
1550 Ils courent. Tout son corps n'est bientôt qu'une plaie.
De nos cris douloureux la plaine retentit.
Leur fougue impétueuse enfin se ralentit.
Ils s'arrêtent, non loin de ces tombeaux antiques,
Où des Rois ses aïeux sont les froides reliques.
J'y cours en soupirant, et sa garde me suit.
De son généreux sang la trace nous conduit.
Les rochers en sont teints. Les ronces dégouttantes
Portent de ses cheveux les dépouilles sanglantes.
J'arrive, je l'appelle, et me tendant la main
1560 Il ouvre un œil mourant, qu'il referme soudain.
Le Ciel, dit-il, *m'arrache une innocente vie.*
Prends soin après ma mort de la triste Aricie.
Cher ami, si mon père un jour désabusé
Plaint le malheur d'un fils faussement accusé,
Pour apaiser mon sang, et mon ombre plaintive,
Dis-lui, qu'avec douceur il traite sa captive,
Qu'il lui rende . . . A ce mot ce héros expiré
N'a laissé dans mes bras qu'un corps défiguré,
Triste objet, où des Dieux triomphe la colère,
1570 Et que méconnaîtrait l'œil même de son père.
    THÉSÉE
O mon fils! cher espoir que je me suis ravi!
Inexorables Dieux, qui m'avez trop servi!
A quels mortels regrets ma vie est réservée!
    THÉRAMÈNE
La timide Aricie est alors arrivée.
Elle venait, Seigneur, fuyant votre courroux,
A la face des Dieux l'accepter pour époux.
Elle approche. Elle voit l'herbe rouge et fumante.
Elle voit (quel objet pour les yeux d'une amante!)
Hippolyte étendu, sans forme et sans couleur.
1580 Elle veut quelque temps douter de son malheur,
Et ne connaissant plus ce héros qu'elle adore,

Of quenchless tears. — I watched, my lord, I watched
Your helpless son dragging behind the steeds
His hands had fed. He tries to call to them,
1570 In vain: his cries startle them. So they gallop
And make one wound of all his living flesh.
    Now as the plain is pealing with our grief
The violent fit is spent. They slacken speed,
And stop, where close at hand his fathers' tombs
And ancient sculptures hold the chill remains
And memories of Kings. I run, behind me
Run all his guard, reading the traces painted
By his gallant blood, past the empurpled crags,
Past dripping brambles hung about with spoils
1580 Of bloody hair. I reach him, I speak; he gives me
A hand and greets me with a dying gaze
That quickly closes. And I hear these words:
    'My guiltless days are forfeit to the Gods.
Do you after my death be watchful over
The sad Aricia; and, sweet friend, if ever
My father undeceived should come to mourn
The misadventure of a slandered son,
To lay in peace my blood and wailing shade
Bid him be gentle to the captive maid,
1590 Render her—' On the word the lifeless youth
Fell back into my arms a ravaged corpse,
The dreadful triumph of an angry Heaven,
Where not a father's eye could undertake
To know his child.

THESEUS

                O child! O dearest hope
I cast away! Gods, ye unswerving Gods,
Too faithfully ye served me! Now must life
Henceforward be a death of long-drawn sorrow.

THERAMENES

And now in fear and haste Aricia,
Stealing, my lord, from your captivity
1600 To hear his nuptial vow before the Gods,
Approached. There are the red and steaming grasses,
And there—what welcome for a bride's regard!—
The hero of her love, but motionless,
Featureless, bloodless. First she seeks to question

Elle voit Hippolyte, et le demande encore.
Mais trop sûre à la fin qu'il est devant ses yeux,
Par un triste regard elle accuse les Dieux,
Et froide, gémissante, et presque inanimée,
Aux pieds de son amant elle tombe pâmée.
Ismène est auprès d'elle. Ismène toute en pleurs
La rappelle à la vie, ou plutôt aux douleurs.
Et moi, je suis venu détestant la lumière
1590 Vous dire d'un héros la volonté dernière,
Et m'acquitter, Seigneur, du malheureux emploi,
Dont son cœur expirant s'est reposé sur moi.
Mais j'aperçois venir sa mortelle ennemie.

SCÈNE DERNIÈRE
THÉSÉE, PHÈDRE, THÉRAMÈNE, PANOPE, GARDES

THÉSÉE
Hé bien vous triomphez, et mon fils est sans vie.
Ah que j'ai lieu de craindre ! Et qu'un cruel soupçon
L'excusant dans mon cœur, m'alarme avec raison !
Mais, Madame, il est mort, prenez votre victime.
Jouissez de sa perte injuste, ou légitime.
Je consens que mes yeux soient toujours abusés,
1600 Je le crois criminel, puisque vous l'accusez.
Son trépas à mes pleurs offre assez de matières,
Sans que j'aille chercher d'odieuses lumières,
Qui ne pouvant le rendre à ma juste douleur,
Peut-être ne feraient qu'accroître mon malheur.
Laissez-moi loin de vous, et loin de ce rivage
De mon fils déchiré fuir la sanglante image.
Confus, persécuté d'un mortel souvenir,
De l'Univers entier je voudrais me bannir.
Tout semble s'élever contre mon injustice.
1610 L'éclat de mon nom même augmente mon supplice.
Moins connu des mortels je me cacherais mieux.
Je hais jusques au soin dont m'honorent les Dieux.
Et je m'en vais pleurer leurs faveurs meurtrières,
Sans plus les fatiguer d'inutiles prières.
Quoi qu'ils fissent pour moi, leur funeste bonté
Ne me saurait payer de ce qu'ils m'ont ôté.

Her misery, and, seeing, still demands
Hippolytus. Then, too pitifully assured,
After one glance reproachful to the skies
Cold, with one cry, lifeless upon the dead
She falls. Ismene, weeping, is beside her
1610 And draws her back to life and life's despair;
And I, still subject to the hostile daylight,
Return to speak a hero's last desires
And so fulfil the grievous ministry
His dying heart committed to my love.
—But here I see the deadliest of his foes.

Enter PHAEDRA, PANOPE, & GUARDS

THESEUS
Well, victory is yours: my son is gone.
Much, much I could suspect; deep rankling doubt
Acquits him in my heart and troubled mind—
But he is dead: your sacrifice, my lady;
1620 Take it, find satisfaction in the forfeit
Unmerited or just. It matters little
That evermore my eyes be blindfolded;
Let him be criminal if you accuse.
His loss alone is theme enough for sorrow,
No need to look for new and fearful knowledge
That, impotent to bring the dead again,
Could pile at most new suffering on the old.
Let me escape, leave you and leave these shores,
Flying the bloody image of a son
1630 Mangled—before that harrying memory
I could long for exile from the world of men.
All things upbraid me, all increase my anguish—
My very name (for nameless, I could hide),
The very honours that the Gods bestowed,
Whose murderous grace I'll mourn, and not again
Importune them with fruitless prayers of mine;
Do what they might, their fatal condescension
Could not console for what they took away.

PHÈDRE

Non, Thésée, il faut rompre un injuste silence ;
Il faut à votre fils rendre son innocence.
Il n'était point coupable.

THÉSÉE

Ah père infortuné !
1620 Et c'est sur votre foi que je l'ai condamné !
Cruelle, pensez-vous être assez excusée . . .

PHÈDRE

Les moments me sont chers, écoutez-moi, Thésée.
C'est moi qui sur ce fils chaste et respectueux
Osai jeter un œil profane, incestueux.
Le Ciel mit dans mon sein une flamme funeste.
La détestable Œnone a conduit tout le reste.
Elle a craint qu'Hippolyte instruit de ma fureur
Ne découvrît un feu qui lui faisait horreur.
La perfide abusant de ma faiblesse extrême
1630 S'est hâtée à vos yeux de l'accuser lui-même.
Elle s'en est punie, et fuyant mon courroux
A cherché dans les flots un supplice trop doux.
Le fer aurait déjà tranché ma destinée.
Mais je laissais gémir la Vertu soupçonnée.
J'ai voulu, devant vous exposant mes remords,
Par un chemin plus lent descendre chez les morts.
J'ai pris, j'ai fait couler dans mes brûlantes veines
Un poison que Médée apporta dans Athènes.
Déjà jusqu'à mon cœur le venin parvenu
1640 Dans ce cœur expirant jette un froid inconnu ;
Déjà je ne vois plus qu'à travers un nuage
Et le ciel, et l'époux que ma présence outrage ;
Et la mort à mes yeux dérobant la clarté
Rend au jour, qu'ils souillaient, toute sa pureté.

PANOPE

Elle expire, Seigneur.

THÉSÉE

D'une action si noire
Que ne peut avec elle expirer la mémoire ?
Allons de mon erreur, hélas ! trop éclaircis
Mêler nos pleurs au sang de mon malheureux fils.
Allons de ce cher fils embrasser ce qui reste,

PHAEDRA

Theseus, I have repented of my silence.
1640 Your son requires his innocence from my lips;
Yes, he was guiltless.

THESEUS

This to me, his father!
And on your solemn faith I sentenced him.
Can any pretext for that cruel act—

PHAEDRA

My time is measured. Listen to me, Theseus.
I, on your dutiful and temperate son,
Looked with profaning and incestuous eyes—
The flame of Heaven lighted in my bosom
A fatal fire. Oenone did the rest;
She feared Hippolytus, my passion known,
1650 Would publish all the madness that he loathed;
Presuming on my feebleness, she came
With that base story of my victim's guilt.
Self-chosen, easy death among the waves
Punished her perfidy and foiled my anger,
And by now the knife would have cleft my destiny,
But goodness still cried out for vindication.
I chose the slower path. I chose to pour
Into your ears before I joined the dead
The chronicle of my remorse. I have drained
1660 And mingled with my burning blood a draught
Medea left in Athens. Now already
Her poison makes its progress toward my heart
Striking that heart with cold it never knew;
Faintly already I perceive the daylight
And you I wound by my unworthy presence;
And death, blurring the sunbeams from these eyes
Whose glance polluted them, restores the light
To perfect purity.

PANOPE

My lord, she is dying

THESEUS

And would the dark remembrance too might die
1670 Of what she has done! Come, all is now too plain.
I must enfold what still remains to touch
Of my dear son, and weeping expiate

1650 Expier la fureur d'un vœu que je déteste.
Rendons-lui les honneurs qu'il a trop mérités.
Et pour mieux apaiser ses mânes irrités,
Que malgré les complots d'une injuste famille
Son amante aujourd'hui me tienne lieu de fille.

FIN

The blind curse I shall evermore bewail
With dear-bought honours rendered at his tomb;
And, better to placate his injured spirit,
I will forget the voice of ancient vengeance
And look upon his lover as my child.

Notes

PREFACE

p.23, l.1 *another tragedy*

After *Iphigénie* (from *Iphigenia in Aulis*), 1664.

p.23, l.6 *the most reasonable thing*

This statement has been diversely interpreted. I suggest (1) that it refers not to the play but to Phaedra's character; (2) that it is explained by the appeal to Aristotle below. The authority of the *Poetics* was accepted because based, so it was considered, on reason.

p.23, l.17 *punishment from the Gods*

The idea that Phaedra is being punished (for some earlier sin) is not in fact present in Racine's play. This phrase has been connected with the Jansenist theology in which Racine was brought up; perhaps wrongly, since no Christian theologian has ever held that God inspires sin. Racine's analysis goes no further than the end of his first act: it is here that the plot parts company with Euripides' (who includes no interview with Hippolytus).

p.25, l.2 *Euripides was blamed* . . .

The only known source for this remark is not classical, but the edition of the *Poetics* by P. Vettori (1560). Vettori, however, goes on to explain that Hippolytus is in fact guilty of *hubris* (commentary on chap. XIII). This looks like special pleading by Racine to excuse the invention of his love for Aricia.

p.25, l.11 *This Aricia*

Seventeenth-century tragedies very commonly contain a character invented by the author to round off the pattern of relationships. Racine often did this: but he takes pride in showing historical or poetic warrant wherever he can.

p.25, l.11 *Vergil relates* . . .

Vergil's words (*Aeneid* VII 761 ff) are ambiguous. One commentator, Servius, thinks the town Aricia is meant.

p.25, l.13 *Aesculapius had brought him back to life*

Cf. Ovid, *Metamorphoses* XV.

p.25, l.14 *in certain authors*

Only sixteenth-century French authorities have been found for the statement that she was Athenian, not Italian.

p.25, l.19 *Plutarch*

Life of Theseus XXX-I, XXXV. This to Racine is history rather than legend.

p.25, l.35 *I have composed none where virtue is shown to more advantage*

This moralizing final paragraph bears all the signs of having been added to reconcile the writer with Christian opinion, at that time hostile to the stage (with which Racine severed his connexion in the same year as *Phèdre* came out). It seems inconsistent with the play: has he not just said that he deliberately made Phaedra *less* odious?

p.27, l.5 *Socrates*

Cf. Diogenes Laërtius, *Life of Socrates*, II 5.

p.27, l.14 *The true purpose of tragedy*

This was an almost universal tenet of the renaissance and the seventeenth century, but will not be found in antiquity.

DRAMATIS PERSONAE

Aricia

Her connexion with the royal line through Pallas (lines 53, 424) is Racine's invention.

Theramenes, Oenone, Ismene, Panope

Fictitious names bestowed by Racine on utility characters, though they are taken from Greek legend or history. For pronunciation, see p.145.

Trozen (for the form see pp.18–19)

Lies opposite Athens on the Saronic Gulf. It was Theseus birthplace. Euripides set his tragedy here, but those of Seneca and his French imitators take place in Athens. Racine's Hippolytus has been relegated here (lines 39–40, 296, 696), and is to inherit it (lines 480–1).

'Stage is a palace with arches. A chair at the beginning.'

(Contemporary notebook of the stage manager at the Hôtel de Bourgogne.)

ACT I

The scene-divisions in the French text are simply a French printers' convention: a scene ends with the entrance or exit of any important character, which is usually indicated only by the list of characters heading the new scene. Action is continuous, except at the ends of acts, when the stage remains empty of actors, and a lapse of time may be supposed to take place if necessary.

Euripides (after his prologue) and Seneca both open their plays with Hippolytus, who dwells on his love of hunting and shows his hate for love. Here that impression is given, then corrected. The modern note is compensated by a wealth of mythological allusions.

12 ff   *Acheron . . .*

The *Acheron*, in Epirus (cf. Preface p.25, l.22, and lines 743, 1000); *Elis* and *Taenarum* (Cape Matapan), in the Peloponnese; the Icarian Sea, off the w coast of Asia Minor (*Icarus*, son of Daedalus, is associated with Cnossos and Pasiphaë).

155   *Enter Phaedra*

This scene follows Euripides (*Hipp.* 176–361) fairly closely up to line 270.

204   *that Barbarian's child*

The argument comes from Euripides, in whose time the son of an Athenian by a non-Athenian woman was considered a bastard. The nurse thinks Hippolytus will be tempted to usurp the throne.

246   *Your trembling knees*

As in Euripides, the nurse performs the ritual gesture of supplication, which cannot be shaken off without impiety.

255   *sister Ariadne*

A tragedy on the abandonment of Ariadne by Theseus on Naxos (cf. lines 91, 657, and Plutarch) had been produced in Racine's theatre in 1672 (*Ariane*, by Corneille's younger brother Thomas).

270   *It was long ago*

For Phaedra's first sight of Hippolytus, and the shrine she builds, Racine has drawn on the prologue spoken by Aphrodite in Euripides (lines 24–33).

283   *I searched the entrails*

She inspected the victims' entrails (like Dido, *Aeneid* IV 64) to see if the gods were favourable to her prayers for composure of mind.

296   *I banished him*

The sending away of Hippolytus is Racine's invention.

351   *Your love* . . .

Oenone is wrong—according to the morality of Racine's day (which he would neither have wished nor dared to flout). Athenian law in Euripides' time permitted marriage with a stepson, but not Christian canon law (cf *I Cor.* 5, 1, and the list of prohibited degrees in the 1662 *Book of Common Prayer*), nor French law. Phaedra never believes Oenone, cf line 714.

363   *ramparts that Minerva reared*

Athens.

A C T I I

473   *Alcides*

Hercules; cf lines 965–6 and Plutarch.

481   *Pittheus*

The father of Theseus' mother.

499   *son of Earth* . . . *Aegeus* . . . *my father*

See genealogical table (p. 146).

Aricia, as daughter (according to Racine) of Pallas, belongs to the direct line, by-passed when Pandion 11 adopted Aegeus. Theseus was son of Aegeus: Hippolytus dutifully justifies his father's kingship by his exceptional services.

573   *has incensed my goddess*

A first declaration of love was a lack of respect, according to the reigning seventeenth-century convention. Commonly the suitor, as Molière's Magdelon admits, 'finds ways of appeasing us later on' (*Précieuses ridicules* sc. iv).

639   *Yes, Prince* . . .

Racine follows Seneca (*Phaedra* 646–62) fairly closely from here to *the thread of life and death* (659). From that point the Roman heroine descends to direct entreaty, and Racine goes his own way.

723   *Give me it*

She snatches it from the scabbard. In Seneca Hippolytus himself draws, but seeing Phaedra eager to die at his hands, flings the sword away (lines 706–14).

A C T I I I

751   *these heralds and these honours*

This is the offer of the crown of Athens (for her son; cf the

previous scene, lines 737 ff). The word 'honours', in English
and French, can = 'regalia'.

815   *ambitious boy*

This is the only hint in the play of their respective ages.
Phaedra, with two infant children, could obviously have been
still very young.

878 ff   *the name I leave* . . .

Phaedra's shame, and her fear of disgracing her children, are
expressed in Euripides (lines 407–25).

904   *Grim as a monster*

She does not say she hates him: she fears him.

931   *his unflinching eyes*

For her acquiescence in the Nurse's false accusation, the final
impulse is given by a mistaken interpretation of Hippolytus'
expression.

936   *No, Theseus* . . .

Words appropriate equally to the true situation and the false
accusation which Phaedra has already authorized. It is uncer-
tain whether we should take this as accidental (and scenes of
cross-purposes are frequent among Racine's contemporaries),
or a result of supreme presence of mind, such as court etiquette
required even in physical extremities.

A C T I V

1023   *What have you said?*

We do not hear Oenone accuse Hippolytus. Racine relegates
the unpleasant episode to the interval between the acts. Her
use of the sword as evidence (cf lines 909 f) is found in Seneca.

1057 ff   *Enter Hippolytus*

The whole confrontation is freely adapted from Euripides
(902 ff). In that play Hippolytus had been sworn to secrecy by
the nurse; in Seneca he does not meet his father. In Racine the
motive for his silence is delicacy of feeling—an 'excess of
generosity' that Dryden considered 'not practicable, but with
fools and madmen' (*All for Love*, preface).

1063 ff   *May I not know* . . .

This question comes more naturally in Euripides, where
Hippolytus has not yet seen his father since the latter's return.

1086   *Neptune*

Cf line 627. Seneca (but not Euripides) adopts the legend
making the god Theseus' father.

1156   *Pillars of Hercules*

Straits of Gibraltar.

1174 *by that River's name*

The Homeric gods swear by the Styx.—By a characteristic Racinian touch, Theseus changes his own state of mind by the force of the words he uses, and begins the slow process of realization of his error which is his nemesis.

1294 *urn*

The detail comes from the *Aeneid*, VI 432.—Minos did become judge of the dead; but Seneca (lines 149 ff) refers to him as still alive and king of Crete. His Phaedra expects punishment after death—a hyperbolical self-denunciation which is fairly common in his characters. It seems doubtful whether an ancient Greek would have thought she deserved it. Vergil shows her after death in company with others who died for love, in the *lugentes campi*—sad but free from torment (*Aen.* VI 445 ff).

1309 *never reaped the sweets*

Critics interpret these words as an impenitent hankering after the sweets of sin; but the context makes it natural to read them as a plea in extenuation of her sin, which, though intended, was never committed in deed.

ACT V

1382 *Most powerful patrons*

Hippolytus plans nothing less than war against his father (because Phaedra's falsehoods have made Theseus act unjustly). It is surprising that he expects aid from other Greek states: but they might be expected to give shelter to Aricia as a legitimate pretender (as France did to the Stuarts).

1411 ff *A wayside temple*

This miraculous temple (to which Hippolytus fails to appeal in defending himself before his father) looks like a hasty expedient by Racine to solve Aricia's dilemma. G. Couton has argued that his audience would recognize the irregular but valid ceremony of marriage *par paroles de présent* in church and before witnesses, but without the intervention of a priest ('Le mariage d'Hippolyte et d'Aricie ou Racine entre Pausanias et le droit canon', *Revue des sciences humaines*, 1963, 305 ff). Marriage in ancient Greece or Rome did involve torches, but not vows nor temples; seventeenth-century dramatists base their descriptions on the (Christian) type of ceremony familiar to their public.

1492 *She takes her children*

Reminiscence of Medea before the murder of her children
(Euripides, *Med.* 1071 ff).

1520 *Still close behind us* . . .

The narrative of Hippolytus' death comes of course in all the
versions; Racine has drawn on Euripides (lines 1173 ff) and
Seneca (lines 1000 ff), but only in his own version does the
hero attack and wound the monster.

1615 ff *But here I see the deadliest of his foes*

This brief finale is Racine's own. The suffering of Theseus is
brought out far more than in the ancient sources; and Phaedra's
death, with the word purity on her lips—in which several
critics have seen an aspiration which is almost a redemption—
is poles apart from her suicide over Hippolytus' mangled remains in Seneca.

1661 *Medea*

After leaving Jason, the magician had come to Athens as wife
of Aegeus, Theseus' father, and had tried to poison Theseus
when he arrived to claim his birthright. (An opera on the
subject, *Thésée*, by Quinault and Lulli, had been acted in Paris
in 1675.)

PRONUNCIATION OF PROPER NAMES (see p. 18)

The symbols used are those of The Concise Oxford Dictionary

Ă'chĕron (-k-)
A̅e̅'ge̅u̅s (ē'jo̅o̅s)
Alcī'dēs (-sī-, not -kē-)
Antĭ'ŏpē
Arĭad'nē
Ărī'cĭa (strictly -rīs-, but
may rhyme with Patricia)
Cer'cy̆on (se̅r̅'sy̆on)
Cōcȳ'tus (kōsī'tus)
Ē'lis
Ēpī'rus
Ērech'the̅u̅s (-rĕk'thyo̅o̅s)
Hĭppŏ'lȳtus
Hȳ'men
Ī'cărus (ī-, not ē-)
Ĭsmē'nē
Mēdē'a

Mī'nos
Mī'nŏtaur
Mȳca̅e̅'na̅e̅ (mīsē'nē)
O̅e̅nō'nē (ē-)
Păn'ŏpē
Pasĭ'phăē (four syllables)
Pĕrĭbo̅e̅'a (-ē-)
Pha̅e̅'dra (-ē-)
Pīrĭ'thŏus (four syllables)
Pĭt'the̅u̅s (or like Matthew)
Prōcrus'tēs
Să'lamis
Scī'ro (sī-)
Sĭn'nis
Ta̅e̅'nărum
Théră'mĕnēs
Thē'se̅u̅s

GENEALOGICAL TABLE OF THE PRINCIPAL CHARACTERS

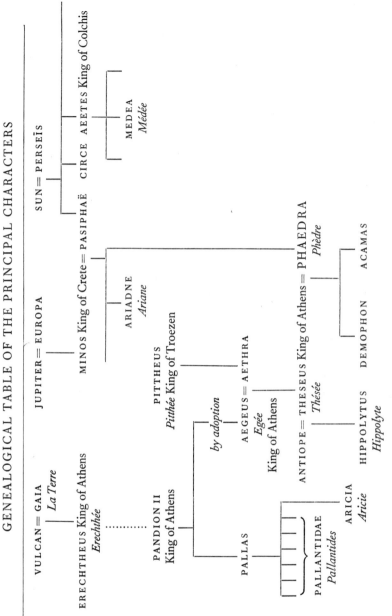